Cliff Herbabee   8-89

BARRON'S BOOK NOTES

Turner

JANE AUSTEN'S

Pride and Prejudice

BY

Ruth Goode

SERIES EDITOR

Michael Spring
Editor, *Literary Cavalcade*
Scholastic Inc.

BARRON'S

BARRON'S EDUCATIONAL SERIES, INC.
Woodbury, New York / London / Toronto / Sydney

ACKNOWLEDGMENTS

We would like to acknowledge the many painstaking hours of work Holly Hughes and Thomas F. Hirsch have devoted to making the *Book Notes* series a success.

All inquiries should be addressed to:
Barron's Educational Series, Inc.
113 Crossways Park Drive
Woodbury, New York 11797

Library of Congress Catalog Card No. 84-18437

International Standard Book No. 0-8120-3437-6

Library of Congress Cataloging in Publication Data
Goode, Ruth.
  Jane Austen's Pride and prejudice.

  (Barrons' book notes)
  Bibliography: p. 94
  Summary: A guide to reading "Pride and Prejudice" with a
critical and appreciative mind. Includes background on
the author's life and times, sample tests, term paper
suggestions, and a reading list.
    1. Austen, Jane, 1775–1817. Pride and prejudice.
  [1. Austen, Jane, 1775–1817. Pride and prejudice.
  2. English literature—History and criticism] I. Title.
  II. Series.
PR4034.P72G66 1984   823'.7   84-18437
ISBN 0-8120-3437-6 (pbk.)

PRINTED IN THE UNITED STATES OF AMERICA

456   550   98765432

CONTENTS

ADVISORY BOARD

HOW TO USE THIS BOOK

You have to know how to approach literature in order to get the most out of it. This *Barron's Book Notes* volume follows a plan based on methods used by some of the best students to read a work of literature.

Begin with the guide's section on the author's life and times. As you read, try to form a clear picture of the author's personality, circumstances, and motives for writing the work. This background usually will make it easier for you to hear the author's tone of voice, and follow where the author is heading.

Then go over the rest of the introductory material—such sections as those on the plot, characters, setting, themes, and style of the work. Underline, or write down in your notebook, particular things to watch for, such as contrasts between characters and repeated literary devices. At this point, you may want to develop a system of symbols to use in marking your text as you read. (Of course, you should only mark up a book you own, not one that belongs to another person or a school.) Perhaps you will want to use a different letter for each character's name, a different number for each major theme of the book, a different color for each important symbol or literary device. Be prepared to mark up the pages of your book as you read. Put your marks in the margins so you can find them again easily.

Now comes the moment you've been waiting for—the time to start reading the work of literature. You may want to put aside your *Barron's Book Notes* volume until you've read the work all the way through. Or you may want to alternate, reading the *Book Notes* analysis of each section as soon as you have finished reading the corresponding part of the original. Before you move on, reread crucial passages you don't fully understand. (Don't take this guide's analysis for granted—make up your own mind as to what the work means.)

Once you've finished the whole work of literature, you may want to review it right away, so you can firm up your ideas about what it means. You may want to leaf through the book concentrating on passages you marked in reference to one character or one theme. This is also a good time to reread the *Book Notes* introductory material, which pulls together insights on specific topics.

When it comes time to prepare for a test or to write a paper, you'll already have formed ideas about the work. You'll be able to go back through it, refreshing your memory as to the author's exact words and perspective, so that you can support your opinions with evidence drawn straight from the work. Patterns will emerge, and ideas will fall into place; your essay question or term paper will almost write itself. Give yourself a dry run with one of the sample tests in the guide. These tests present both multiple-choice and essay questions. An accompanying section gives answers to the multiple-choice questions as well as suggestions for writing the essays. If you have to select a term paper topic, you may choose one from the list of suggestions in this book. This guide also provides you with a reading list, to help you when you start research for a term paper, and a selection of provocative comments by critics, to spark your thinking before you write.

THE AUTHOR AND HER TIMES

Jane Austen was a country parson's daughter who lived most of her life in a tiny English village. She began writing her first novel, *Sense and Sensibility*, when she was still in her late teens. When she wrote the original version of her second and most famous novel, *Pride and Prejudice* (originally entitled *First Impressions*), she was not yet twenty-one. At that time she had never been away from home, except for a few years at a girls' boarding school before the age of ten. And yet, although she had seen almost nothing of the world beyond Steventon, the town where she grew up, she was able to write a witty, worldly novel of love, money, and marriage.

Jane Austen's world seems very narrow to us today. The year she was born, 1775, was an important one in English as well as American history, but to the people of the little village of Steventon, the American Revolution was something very far away that hardly touched their lives at all. Years later while Austen was writing her novels, England was involved in the Napoleonic Wars, but you won't find much mention of them in her work. One reason these wars did not affect the English at home very much was that they were fought entirely on foreign soil or at sea, and they did not involve very large numbers of Englishmen. (Two of Jane Austen's brothers did see combat as naval officers and both reached the rank of admiral, and a naval officer who did well in the wars is one of her most attractive heroes in her last novel, *Persua-*

sion.) Another reason is that—without television, radio, telephones, automobiles, or even railroads—news traveled slowly.

People traveled very little, and when they did it was on foot, by public coach, or—if they could afford it—by private carriage. In the evenings they sat together around the fire, mother and girls mending or embroidering by candlelight and often someone reading aloud. For entertainment, they might visit a neighbor or go to a dance in the village public hall. At these so-called assemblies, young people were chaperoned by mothers and aunts, and only the most correct behavior was tolerated. If there was a large estate in the neighborhood, the squire or lord of the manor would give evening parties and occasionally a ball, to which his lady would invite the leading families of the countryside.

Jane Austen wrote *Pride and Prejudice* in the family sitting room while her six brothers and a sister, her father's pupils, and visiting neighbors swirled around her. She would cover her manuscript with a blotter during interruptions and take up her pen again when the room was quiet. All the while, she was watching, listening, and thinking about the world around her. The novel reflects her understanding of and active involvement with "ordinary" people.

The plot of *Pride and Prejudice* is based on the concerns of people in early nineteenth-century country society. One of these concerns is money. Austen could observe the money problems of a middle-class family right in her own home. As a clergyman of the Church of England, her father was an educated man and a gentleman. But his parish consisted of only about three hundred people, and his income didn't provide well for his family, so he had to take in students in addition to his church duties. Even so, he could send only one son, the oldest, to Oxford, and he couldn't give his daughters attractive dowries or an income if they remained unmarried.

Like other young women of their social class, Jane and her sister Cassandra were educated, mostly at home, in the "ladylike" subjects of music, drawing and painting, needlework, and social behavior. Thanks to her father and her own literary tastes, Jane was also very well read. Tall and graceful, with dark hair and beautiful hazel eyes, she enjoyed parties, liked to dance, and had numerous suitors. As it turned out, however, neither Jane nor her sister Cassandra ever married. After their father died in 1805, they and their mother were cared for by a brother who had been adopted by a wealthy childless couple and had inherited a sizable estate. (Such adoptions were a fairly common custom of the time.)

Such realities of middle-class life are central to *Pride and Prejudice*. Critics of a hundred or so years ago called Jane Austen "vulgar" and "mercenary," because she writes so frankly about money. One of the first things we learn about her characters, for example, is how much income they have. Her critics considered it bad taste to talk about money, either one's own or someone else's.

But in the middle class of Jane Austen's time, the amount of your income could be a matter of life and death. What is more, it was not money you worked for and earned that mattered, but money you were born to or inherited. People who worked—businessmen, manufacturers, and even some professional people, such as lawyers—were not accepted as members of the "gentry." They were "in trade," and the gentry looked down on them.

While Austen was writing, a great change was coming over England. The industrial revolution was reaching its height, and a new middle class of prosperous factory owners was developing. Yet in the midst of this change, one ancient English tradition still survived, and that was that the true gentry were not the newly rich in the cities but those who lived on their inherited estates. The new middle class, who had become rich "in trade," were therefore buying manor houses and estates in the country, and setting up their heirs as members of the landed aristocracy.

In *Pride and Prejudice* the two leading male characters represent this social change. Mr. Darcy's aristocratic family goes back for generations, and he draws his income from his vast estate of tenant farms. His friend Mr. Bingley, however, is heir to a fortune made "in trade" and is looking for a suitable country estate to establish himself in the upper class.

Notice how different characters in the novel react to these social distinctions. Jane Austen herself, through her heroine Elizabeth, expresses her contempt for snobbery. You'll find that she pokes fun at the snobs and makes them her most comical characters.

Still, there was a very serious side to all this, and that was the situation of young women. In our time, women have many other choices in addition to marriage. In Jane Austen's time it wasn't so. A young woman of her class depended for her happiness, her health, in fact the whole shape of her life, on her making a good marriage. If her husband was poor or a gambler or a drunkard, she and her children could suffer genuine privation. A girl with no fortune of her own often could not attract a husband. Then she might have to become a governess, living in other people's houses, looking after their children and subject to their whims.

The necessity of making a good marriage is one of the major themes of *Pride and Prejudice*, but that doesn't mean the novel is old fashioned. In fact, you may find that you can make a good argument for calling Jane Austen a feminist and her novel a feminist novel. It's a serious novel in many ways, but also a very funny one.

Jane Austen began writing novels simply to entertain herself and her family, with no idea of having her stories published. In her time, novels weren't considered a respectable form of literature, rather the way murder mysteries and Gothic romances are looked down on in our own time. Ministers preached and social critics thundered against the habit of reading novels. Meanwhile, hundreds of novels were being published—most of them trashy romances or wildly exaggerated adventure yarns—and people went right on reading them.

Most of these novels, including some of the better ones, were written by women. Writing was one of the few possible occupations for an intelligent, educated woman. Women could write at home while fulfilling their traditional role of running a household and bringing up children. They could stay out of the public eye, hiding behind an assumed name. George Eliot's real name was Mary Ann Travers, the Brontë sisters wrote under the name of Bell, and George Sand in real life was Madame Dudevant. When Jane Austen's books were finally published, thanks to her brother Henry who acted as her agent, the title page just said "By a Lady." Her novels were read by a small, exclusive audience during her lifetime. She lived a quiet life and never yearned for celebrity.

Austin was working on her sixth and last novel, *Persuasion*, when Henry fell ill and she moved to London to nurse him. Soon afterward her own health began to fail. With Cassandra as her nurse and companion, she moved to Winchester to be treated by a famous surgeon there. He apparently could not help her, and on July 18, 1817, she died, just five months short of her forty-second birthday.

Judging from her letters, which radiate good humor and laugh off minor misfortunes, Jane Austen's life, although short, was a busy and contented one. If the lively, witty Elizabeth Bennet in *Pride and Prejudice* was modeled on any living person, the model must have been Jane Austen herself.

THE NOVEL

The Plot

In the neighborhood of the Bennet family's estate of Longbourn, Mr. Bingley, an attractive young bachelor with a good income, has moved into the nearby manor. He falls in love with the oldest of the five Bennet daughters, Jane. But his friend, wealthy and aristocratic Mr. Darcy, disapproves of Bingley's choice. Darcy considers the Bennet family to be socially inferior, and he plots with Bingley's sisters to separate the lovers. Meanwhile, though, Darcy is finding it hard to resist his own increasing attraction to Jane's next younger sister, the vivacious Elizabeth.

Elizabeth is prejudiced against Darcy because he seems so proud and conceited. She also suspects that he has interfered between Jane and Bingley. She is even more put off when she hears that Darcy has treated a young man, George Wickham, cruelly and unjustly. Wickham tells her that Darcy has denied him the inheritance that his godfather, Darcy's father, left him. Wickham courts Elizabeth, and his good looks, charming manners, and story of injustice at Darcy's hands win her sympathy and deepen her prejudice against Darcy.

Because Mr. Bennet has no son, his estate will be inherited by his nearest male relative, Mr. Collins. This pompous clergyman comes to Longbourn seeking a wife. He proposes to Elizabeth, who rejects him—even though marrying him would be the one way to keep Longbourn in the family. But he wins her best friend, Charlotte Lucas, a plain young woman who marries Collins to escape from spinsterhood into a safe, if loveless, marriage.

The story continues with an interweaving of plot and subplots. Elizabeth visits Charlotte, now Mrs. Collins. Darcy visits his aunt, Lady Catherine, who is Mr. Collins's patron. Darcy and Elizabeth meet constantly, and at last he proposes to her, saying with more honesty than tact that he does this against his better judgment. She angrily rejects him, accusing him of destroying Jane's happiness and Wickham's legitimate prospects. Later, in an earnest letter, he tells her the truth on both counts: he did interfere between Jane and Bingley, but he did not treat Wickham unjustly. In fact, he says, Wickham is a thoroughly bad character. Elizabeth believes Darcy for once, and her prejudice against him begins to weaken.

Elizabeth goes on a trip with her aunt and uncle, the Gardiners. They come to Darcy's magnificent estate in his absence and are shown through the house. His housekeeper praises him for his goodness and generosity, painting a very different picture of him from the one Elizabeth has had. Suddenly and unexpectedly, Darcy himself arrives. Elizabeth is mortified to be found there, but he is full of courtesy to the Gardiners and very attentive to Elizabeth.

Bad news comes from Longbourn: The youngest Bennet girl, giddy sixteen-year-old Lydia, has run away with Wickham. Such a scandal must disgrace the whole family, and Elizabeth decides that now, just as her feelings toward Darcy have begun to change, any hope of his renewing his proposal is lost forever.

But not so. Darcy feels partially responsible for Lydia's elopement; he feels he should have warned the Bennets that Wickham once tried the same thing with Darcy's own sister. Besides, he is very much in love with Elizabeth. For her sake he searches out the fugitive couple, makes sure that they are legally married, pays Wickham's debts, and buys him a commission in the army. All this he does secretly. But, though sworn to secrecy, Lydia reveals Darcy's part in her rescue—and Elizabeth realizes at last how wrong she's been about him all along.

Bingley, with Darcy's encouragement, proposes to Jane and is accepted. Soon Darcy makes his proposal again to Elizabeth. By now she has abandoned her prejudice and he has subdued his pride, and so they are married and all ends happily.

The Characters

MAJOR CHARACTERS

Elizabeth Bennet

The leading female character in the novel is just under twenty-one. She is not as beautiful as her older sister but pretty enough, with fine eyes and a light, graceful figure. Mr. Darcy is attracted by her looks, but he especially likes what he calls her "lively mind"—she herself calls it her "impertinence." She is quick to make fun of people's absurdities and hypocrisies, but she's also deeply serious about some things—particularly about people's power to make each other happy or unhappy. This seriousness is the main source of her prejudice against Darcy, and also—when she learns more about him—the source of her love for him. Unlike Jane, she is quick to express her feelings; she is fiery in expressing her anger at Darcy for what she believes he has done to make Jane unhappy and to ruin Wickham's prospects. She also tries to persuade her father that he must be firm with Lydia, but she fails to budge him. She is too loyal to criticize her father openly, but she admits to herself that he is wrong in his treatment both of Lydia and of his wife.

Fitzwilliam Darcy

Darcy is the leading male character in the novel, a tall, handsome man of twenty-eight, who first scorns and then falls in love with Elizabeth, much against his will. Unlike his friend Bingley, who is delighted with the friendly country society, Darcy's first impression is that there is no one attractive enough to dance with or even talk to. Even Elizabeth seems to him merely "tolerable" when he first sees her. His ancient family name, magnificent estate, and sizable fortune all contribute to his pride. But there's another side to his character, as Elizabeth and we, the readers, learn. He is a generous master to his servants and tenants and a loving brother to his young sister Georgiana. He is so steadfast in his love for Elizabeth—even though she has rejected him,—that he finds and rescues her sister from disgrace. He does this in secret, not expecting even to be thanked for it. He is too honorable to win Elizabeth's hand by this unselfish action alone. He does not want her gratitude; he wants her love. Darcy's character gradually unfolds in the course of the story, and we, along with Elizabeth, like him better the more sides of him we see. We also see that he takes Elizabeth's criticism of him to heart—makes an effort to curb his pride and judge people according to what they really are, not merely by their rank in society. He demonstrates this change by his politeness and then his growing friendship with Elizabeth's aunt and uncle, the Gardiners, even though Mr. Gardiner is "in trade." The gradual revelation and development of Darcy's character—from pride to generosity and gentleness—is one of the strengths of the novel.

Jane Bennet

Elizabeth's older sister is in her early twenties. She is the family beauty, and she is also the sweetest-natured of the family. She can't see anybody's faults and is never cross or angry. Her calmness and even temper turn out to be a disadvantage to her, however, when she doesn't seem to return Bingley's affection and he is easily discouraged from proposing to her. Although Jane hides her feelings from most people, Elizabeth knows that she really loves Bingley and suffers at losing him.

Charles Bingley

Darcy's friend provides a contrast to Darcy the way Jane provides contrast to Elizabeth. Where Darcy is proud and hard to please, Bingley is easygoing and ready to like everybody. He is also good-looking and a highly eligible bachelor. As the heir to a fortune, he is looking for a country estate, but he is taking his time and enjoying his freedom. Although he is attractive, he is unsure of himself and quick to believe Darcy when Darcy says that Jane Bennet doesn't love him. When Darcy changes his opinion of the situation, Bingley just as readily renews his attentions to Jane and wins her hand. As Elizabeth says, from Darcy's point of view Bingley is a most convenient friend, so willing to be led in the way that Darcy wants him to go.

Caroline Bingley

Charles's sister is a fashionable young woman and what we today would call a social climber. She would like to forget that her own and her brother's fortunes were made "in trade" and is ambitious to step up higher in society by way of marriage. When Charles seems interested in Jane Bennet, Caroline pretends to be friendly to her, but she lets Jane know that she hopes her brother will marry Darcy's sister. She also conspires with Darcy to separate her brother from Jane. As for Elizabeth, Caroline is barely polite to her face and critical, even spiteful, behind her back. She is obviously jealous of Darcy's growing interest in Elizabeth. She herself had hoped to marry him.

Mr. Bennet

Elizabeth's father is a witty, scholarly country gentleman whose comments and opinions contribute much to the comedy of the novel. But he is also a disappointed man, who long ago gave up all hope of finding happiness in his marriage—and who treats his foolish wife and younger daughters as objects of amusement. He loves his two older girls, Jane and Elizabeth (Elizabeth is his favorite). But his unwillingness to control his wife's silly talk and his youngest daughter Lydia's flirtatious behavior comes close to wrecking both Jane's and Elizabeth's hopes of making happy marriages. Another of his disappointments is that his estate is entailed—meaning that it can go only to a male heir—and he has no son. Like most human beings, he would like to avoid unpleasantness, particularly the unpleasantness of having to save money and provide for the future. In his early years, always expecting the birth of a boy, he saw no need to save any of his income in order to provide for his daughters' future. By the time the fifth Bennet baby turned out to be still another girl, it seemed to him too late to do anything about the situation. Elizabeth loves her father dearly, but even she can't pretend that he doesn't have these serious faults as a husband and father.

Mrs. Bennet

Elizabeth's mother is a figure of fun from the very opening scene of the novel; the fact is that she is really not very bright. Her whole purpose in life is to get her daughters married, but her lack of sense and judgment goes far to damage their prospects. She babbles constantly, complains of her nerves, and takes to her bed when things go wrong. She is even more embarrassing to her two older daughters when she is in good spirits, making silly comments and boasting loudly of their expectations. Her indulgence of Lydia's wildness carries the family to the brink of disaster.

Lydia Bennet

The youngest daughter is a feather-brained sixteen-year-old interested only in bonnets, balls, and flirting with the officers stationed in town. She is not beautiful, but her youth and high spirits make her attractive—she is probably much like what Mrs. Bennet was at that age. Like her mother, she has little common sense, no judgment of right and wrong, and no understanding of the suffering her thoughtless behavior causes her family, particularly her older sisters. Both she and Mrs. Bennet take pride in the fact that Lydia is the first of the girls to be married, with no thought at all of the circumstances of the marriage, the character of her husband, and the poor prospects for their future happiness.

Mary Bennet

Mary is the middle sister, a plain, bookish girl given to showing off her muscial accomplishments, much to Elizabeth's embarrassment.

Catherine Bennet

Kitty, as she is called, is older than Lydia but trails after her and shares in the younger girl's misadventures.

George Wickham

Wickham first comes on the scene as the most attractive man Elizabeth has ever met. When he pays attention to her, she is too flattered to be suspicious of how much he is confiding in someone he hardly knows. He tells her about growing up on the Darcy estate, where his father was Darcy's father's steward. He claims that after Darcy's father's death, Darcy refused to provide for him as the elder Darcy had wished. Considering how Elizabeth already feels about Darcy, she is all too ready to believe and sympathize with Wickham. Like most people, she is eager to like and think the best of someone who shows that he likes her, no matter what her judgment might otherwise tell her. She is so prejudiced—against Darcy and in Wickham's favor—that she doesn't doubt Wickham's story for a moment. In fact, however, Wickham is the only real villain in the novel. He is a gambler and fortune hunter, forever in debt and forever seeking to marry a girl with money. As Elizabeth later learns, he once tried to elope with Darcy's sister, an heiress. When he runs away with Elizabeth's sister Lydia, he is in fact running away to escape his debts, and he lets Lydia come along—not because he cares for her, but because she wants to go with him and he doesn't mind having a female companion.

As you read the novel, ask yourself to what degree Wickham's character is the result of his position in society. As an estate steward's son, he was only a little higher in social rank than a farmer, but Darcy's father was fond of him and gave him the education of a gentleman. This raised his expectations and gave him a taste for high living. He tells Elizabeth that Darcy was jealous of his father's affection for him. In fact, Wickham has always been—understandably—jealous of Darcy, who was born to wealth and status. Of course Wickham could have made a life for himself as a clergyman, which was the future that Darcy's father foresaw for him, or in the army, which would have been more to his own taste. But his appetite for pleasure and excitement, so much like Lydia's, makes it certain that he will never behave in a mature, responsible way.

NOTE: By running off with Lydia, Wickham seems at first to have destroyed all hope of happiness for both Jane and Elizabeth. In the end, though, his behavior actually helps bring both pairs of lovers together—thanks to Jane Austen's skill with characters and plot.

Reverend William Collins

Mr. Bennet's cousin and heir to the Longbourn estate is one of Jane Austen's great comic creations. He is an example of how she expressed her criticisms of society through humor. Mr. Collins is pompous, pretentious, and obviously hypocritical in his moral judgments; and he takes every opportunity to flatter and win the approval of his social superiors. He comes to Longbourn in search of a wife, a well-meaning attempt to compensate the Bennets by keeping the estate in the family. But of course Elizabeth won't have him, so he sneaks off across the fields to Lucas Lodge to try for Charlotte, who needs no coaxing to accept him. As you will see, Collins's meddling in the Bennet family's affairs is not only a source of comedy; it also—ironically—helps to bring Elizabeth and Darcy together.

Charlotte Lucas

Elizabeth's best friend is intelligent but plain. Like Elizabeth and Jane, she has no fortune of her own; unlike them, she has little chance of attracting a husband of her own choosing. Charlotte shocks Elizabeth by accepting a proposal of marriage from the ridiculous Mr. Collins. Marriage to this foolish, pompous man cannot promise companionship—let alone love—but it does promise security, and that is enough for Charlotte. In her opinion, happiness in marriage is all a matter of chance. In the character of Charlotte, Jane Austen gives us a picture of the reality that the ordinary young woman of her class had to face. While Jane with her beauty and Elizabeth with her wit and charm might win a good man's love, a plain, sensible girl like Charlotte could only try to achieve security and perhaps some comfort in a home of her own.

Lady Catherine de Bourgh

Darcy's aunt and Mr. Collins's patron, is another of Austen's comic creations. She is a bossy woman who considers it her duty to look into people's affairs and tell them how to manage their lives. She visits Elizabeth for the sole purpose of getting her to promise not to marry Mr. Darcy. In the end, though, her interference—and her report to Darcy of Elizabeth's response to it—give Darcy the courage to propose again.

Mr. and Mrs. Gardiner

Elizabeth's uncle and aunt, are Jane Austen's answer to the snobs she makes fun of in the novel. Mr. Gardiner is "in trade" and the Gardiner home is in an unfashionable part of London. But the Gardiner's are as well bred as the born gentry and have better manners than some titled folk—for example Darcy's own aunt, Lady Catherine de Bourgh. Edward Gardiner is Mrs. Bennet's brother, but he is nothing like her. He is a sensible, dignified, and responsible gentleman. His wife is fashionable in a quiet way, and a loving adviser to Elizabeth and Jane. The Gardiners bring Elizabeth and Darcy together by chance, and Darcy's politeness to her uncle and aunt lets Elizabeth know that he still cares for her and that he realizes not all of her family are like her mother and younger sisters. The Gardiners are the ones to whom Darcy turns for help in rescuing Lydia, and it is from Mrs. Gardiner that Elizabeth finally learns of Darcy's generosity on behalf of her family.

MINOR CHARACTERS

Miss De Bourgh
Lady Catherine's daughter.

Georgiana Darcy
Darcy's sister.

Sir William and Lady Lucas
Charlotte Lucas's parents.

Mr. and Mrs. Philips
Mrs. Bennet's sister and brother-in-law.

Mr. and Mrs. Hurt
Bingley's married sister and her husband.

Other Elements

SETTING

Jane Austen sets her novel in places she was probably familiar with as a girl. Mr. Bennet's modest gentleman's estate is the main setting with excursions to (a) Meryton, a provincial town within walking distance where a regiment of militia is the chief attraction for the younger Bennet girls; and (b) the more distant and far grander Pemberley, Mr. Darcy's inherited manor in Derbyshire. Some action takes place in the more modest manor house of Netherfield. Rented by Mr. Bingley, Netherfield is located in the neighborhood of the Bennet home of Longbourn.

Although never specifically described, the various rooms in which the Bennet family live and entertain their visitors, the surrounding gardens where they walk, and the farm that provides their income, all become familiar to us. So does the main street of Meryton where the Bennet girls encounter the officers on their walks and their Aunt Philips keeps track of comings and goings from her window.

The only setting that is described in detail is Pemberley. There the beauty of every view and the good taste of every rich furnishing become part of the developing love story of Elizabeth and Darcy. You can see the novelist's skillful hand here, in the economy with which she uses the physical description of this setting both to unfold significant aspects of her hero's character and to advance her plot.

THEME

How to get a husband, and preferably a rich one, is the central theme of the novel. Austen's concern with money has won her the accusation of being vulgar and mercenary. Yet in her hands, under the guise of comedy, the subject is transformed into a serious and sympathetic exposure of the lot of women in her society. For the women of her time marriage on any terms was often the only escape from a depressing spinsterhood in respectable poverty. Around this crucial issue of marriage she weaves her lively subthemes of social criticism, making fun of snobbery, hypocrisy, the spiteful gossip of respectable housewives and the prying impertinence of ladies of title. While the drive of her story is getting the Bennet girls married, Austen incidentally examines marriage itself, and its effect on five different couples. She comments, through her heroine, on the ironic fact that the Bennets must be happy over a marriage (Lydia's to Wickham) that can bring no happiness to anyone. Here is a brief look at some of the subthemes:

1. GOOD MANNERS

Every society has its rules of social behavior, but manners are much less important today than they were in Jane Austen's time. Her world was dominated by social rituals that had built-in rules—balls, formal visits, and conversations in which people were supposed to avoid personal or otherwise embarrassing subjects. In *Pride and Prejudice* Austen demonstrates her view that these rules are necessary: they constitute civil and considerate behavior, the "oil" that allows relationships to run smoothly. She is often critical of characters who break the rules and sometimes uses them for comic effect—as when Lady Catherine de Bourgh pries into the Bennet family's affairs. Mr. Collins represents the other side of the coin—he is comic because he carries good manners to a ridiculous extreme. Elizabeth represents the middle ground. When Mr. Collins proposes, she rejects him with a proper "thank you." But when Darcy proposes, she tells him that she cannot express gratitude to him because she does not *feel* gratitude—and she goes on to tell him exactly how she does feel, in words that bristle with angry criticism of him. It is clear that while Jane Austen approves of the correct forms of social behavior, she makes fun of them when they are carried to excess, and she does not approve of them as cover-ups of strong and justifiable feelings.

2. PRIVILEGE AND RESPONSIBILITY

The English gentry, as Jane Austen shows us, were highly privileged people. When Darcy is criticized for being proud, Charlotte Lucas comes to his defense, saying that a man of his wealth and family background has a right to be proud. As the story unfolds, however, it becomes clear that privilege brings with it responsibilities—ones that Darcy takes seriously. For example, his housekeeper tells of his generous treatment of his servants and tenants. And, shortly after that, Darcy undertakes the rescue of Lydia and the rehabilitation of Wickham, at least as far as he is able. Darcy's sense of responsibility impresses Elizabeth and finally wipes away her prejudice against him.

3. RELATIONSHIPS

Jane Austen is known for her preceptive depiction of relationships. In *Pride and Prejudice*, for example, she shows us all kinds of marriages, no two of them alike: Mr. and Mrs. Bennet, Charlotte and Mr. Collins, Lydia and Wickham, Jane and Bingley, and, finally, Elizabeth and Darcy. She also shows us other kinds of relationships: the sisterly relationship of Jane and Elizabeth, the aunt and niece relationship of Elizabeth and Mrs. Gardiner. Finally, there are the friendships: Elizabeth and Charlotte enjoy a friendship of equals, even though they do not always agree. Darcy and Bingley, on the other hand, have an odd relationship in which Bingley confesses himself to be in awe of Darcy, and Darcy, the stronger character, has taken on a responsibility for his friend's welfare—to the point of manipulating him away from courting Jane.

At the end of the novel, when Darcy and Elizabeth are married, Darcy's sister Georgiana is amazed that Elizabeth can tease Darcy and make him laugh at himself—a privilege, as Jane Austen points out, that a wife may have but not a younger sister. In this final subtle touch Jane Austen shows her mastery of the art of relationships.

STYLE

Jane Austen's graceful, economical narrative style was unique in her time. It was an era in literature given to flowery wordiness and emotional excess. Readers of the day could take their choice among collections of sermons to improve their minds, tales of sin and punishment to improve their morals, and horror stories to stimulate their circulation. *Pride and Prejudice* is told in a readable prose without a single superfluous word, and it frequently breaks into dialogue so lively and so revealing of characters that entire scenes have been lifted bodily from the novel and reproduced in dramatized versions for stage and screen. In some passages the author enters into the mind of one or another of her characters, most often into her heroine Elizabeth's, and there she reveals her character's capacity for humor and self-criticism. Austen's style is so deceptively lucid that we can hardly believe she submitted her writing to so much polishing and revision.

POINT OF VIEW

Pride and Prejudice is mostly written from the objective view of an external observer. However, from time to time the novel departs from this objective storytelling approach to explore the thoughts and feelings of a character—either Darcy as he slips little by little into love with Elizabeth, or Elizabeth as she considers her own behavior and the behavior of others. Whatever the approach whether through Elizabeth's mind or through the voice of a narrator, the point of view is always and unmistakably Jane Austen's. It is always her sharply critical eye, youthful though it was when she wrote the novel, that observes and subtly comments on her society's follies and foibles, making us laugh but also making us aware. When we finish her book we know very well the defects she saw in the people of her world, but we also know how much she enjoyed her life among them, faults and all.

FORM AND STRUCTURE

Like her writing style, the structure of Jane Austen's novel is deceptively simple. She appears to be telling a straightforward story, character by character and happening by happening, exactly as it occurred in chronological sequence. We can in fact read the novel that way. But on closer look we find that *Pride and Prejudice* is not merely a record of events. Instead, it is an interweaving of plot and sub-plots, an intricate pattern with various threads.

The main plot follows the far from smooth course of the romance between Elizabeth and Darcy and the conflict of his pride and her prejudice. Their feelings, born of first impressions, are not the only obstacles between them. Three sub-plots complicate their relationship.

The first is Bingley's attraction to Jane Bennet and Darcy's intervention to save his friend from what he sees as an undesirable marriage. The second is Wickham's involvement with the Darcy family, and his ability to charm Elizabeth and deepen her prejudice against Darcy. The third is Charlotte Lucas' marriage to Mr. Collins, which throws Elizabeth and Darcy together and sharpens their differences.

Elizabeth ends up rejecting Darcy in what we come to see as the first dramatic climax of the story. The Wickham sub-plot brings on the second dramatic climax: his elopement with Lydia and the scandal and probable ruin of the entire Bennet family.

Austen maintains an air of suspense to the very end. She also keeps her three sub-plots alive with a novelist's juggling skill. In the end, all three sub-plots contribute to the resolution of the principal plot, and the hero and heroine come together in happiness at last.

The Story

CHAPTER ONE

"It is a truth universally acknowledged that a single man in possession of a good fortune must be in want of a wife."

This opening line of *Pride and Prejudice* has become one of the most famous sentences in English literature. With this single short statement, Jane Austen does three things:

1. She declares one of her major themes: Money and Marriage.

2. She establishes an ironic, humorous tone by using very intellectual-sounding words to introduce a subject that is not intellectual at all—the search for someone to marry.

3. She sets the stage for a chase—either by the young man in search of a bride, or by young women in pursuit of him as a husband.

As we all know from reading adventure stories or watching slapstick movie comedies, a chase can be one of the most entertaining forms of narrative. Jane Austen seemed to know that too, because from the opening scene that follows her first sentence, the chase is on.

Mrs. Bennet tells her husband that a single young man, Mr. Bingley, has rented the nearby manor house of Netherfield. She is sure that he will fall in love with one of the Bennet daughters, and tells Mr. Bennet that he must begin the acquaintance at once by calling on him. Mr. Bennet teases her by saying she should send her daughters themselves over to Mr.

Bingley so that he can get a good look at them. She is offended at the suggestion and complains of her poor nerves. Mrs. Bennet never knows when her husband is making fun of her.

NOTE: The opening scene of the novel is written almost entirely in dialogue. This is the way Jane Austen develops both her characters and her story. She does not tell, she *shows*. *Pride and Prejudice* has been successfully adapted for three forms of the drama—stage, motion pictures, and television—and you can see why just from this first scene. If you were to make a note of similar scenes as they occur, you'd see that by assembling them you'd have the whole action of the novel in dramatic form. One of the most entertaining ways to enjoy and understand the novel is to read some of these scenes aloud or even act them out.

The short first chapter makes clear in a few lines of dialogue the relationship of Elizabeth's parents and the quality of their marriage. Most of the novel is about young women hoping to get married, yet here at the very start of the story we find a couple who are not a good example of happiness in marriage. In the course of the novel, Austen shows how several other marriages work. Some are happy, some not, and no two are alike. In a society in which marriage was so important to women—and to men—the qualities that make a marriage succeed are quite a serious matter. Austen treats the subject with comedy, but underneath the comic surface she is very serious. Notice, as you read, what qualities she shows us as good and bad in a marriage.

CHAPTER TWO

In another scene of domestic comedy, Mr. Bennet is teasing his wife again, but by this time he has done his social duty and introduced himself to Bingley. Mrs. Bennet expresses her joy in the same way she expressed her disappointment earlier—excessively. She is already planning when she can invite the newcomer to dinner.

CHAPTER THREE

Mr. Bingley returns Mr. Bennet's visit, but he does not see the young ladies. They, however, try to watch him from an upstairs window, although all they can see is that he wears a blue coat and rides a black horse.

NOTE: By having the sisters watch Bingley from a window, Austen shows us how restricted they are, compared with the young men such as Bingley, who have much more freedom.

The girls are dying to know what Mr. Bingley is like. Mr. Bennet can't be bothered with what he considers silly questions. But their neighbor, Lady Lucas, comes calling, and she tells them what her husband has told her about Mr. Bingley. He seems to fulfill all their hopes. He's young, handsome, and friendly—and he'll be bringing several gentlemen and ladies to the next village ball.

In a quick transition, we are at the ball. Mr. Bingley arrives with his two sisters, the husband of one of them, and Bingley's aristocratic friend, Mr. Darcy. Rumor runs swiftly around the assembly room: tall, handsome Mr. Darcy is twice as rich as Mr. Bingley and owns a large estate in Derby shire.

NOTE: How much money Darcy has is the first fact we learn about him. Is that usually the first thing we want to know about a person? Do you think the people in Jane Austen's time and social class were more mercenary than we are today? More realistic? Or was a person's income really the most important thing about him? One thing we can say for sure is that in Austen's time—even more than in our own—the amount of money a person's family had determined that person's rank in society. To know a person's income therefore gave a very good idea of how that person stood in the world.

All too soon, Darcy offends the company by his proud and disdainful manners. While Bingley dances every dance (and two dances with Jane Bennet, as everybody notices), Darcy dances once with each of the ladies in his own group and refuses to be introduced to any others. He gives the cold shoulder to Elizabeth, telling Bingley, "She is tolerable, but not handsome enough to tempt *me*." Elizabeth overhears this remark and repeats it as a funny story, so that we can't tell whether her feelings are hurt, or whether she has already written Darcy off as too disagreeable to be bothered with.

NOTE: With a few quick strokes of dialogue and action, this scene sets up several contrasts: Bingley's attitudes are contrasted to Darcy's; Jane's personality is contrasted to Elizabeth's. What's more, two beginning love affairs are contrasted: While the romance of Jane and Bingley starts smoothly, Elizabeth and Darcy manage to antagonize each other from the very beginning. We can look forward to seeing them strike sparks from each other whenever they meet.

CHAPTER FOUR

In the privacy of their room, Jane confesses to Elizabeth how much she admires Bingley and likes his sisters. Elizabeth teases her about Bingley but says nothing about his sisters—even though she finds them haughty, conceited, and insincere. This is the first time that we see Elizabeth holding back some knowledge or observation from Jane; it won't be the last. Elizabeth may laugh at Jane sometimes, or tease her into laughing at herself when she becomes too serious, but she is also careful to protect Jane from anything that will hurt her gentle sister's feelings.

The scene at Longbourn is mirrored in one at Netherfield, where Bingley and Darcy also rehash the ball and where opinions also differ. To Bingley, everyone at the party was delightful and Miss Jane Bennet in particular is an angel, while to Darcy it was a company that had no fashion and little beauty. He admits that Miss Bennet is pretty, but in his opinion she smiles too much. Bingley's sisters tell him she is a sweet girl.

NOTE: The original title of *Pride and Prejudice* was "First Impressions." As you read the novel, decide how accurate the characters' first impressions of each other were—and watch how their attitudes change.

CHAPTER FIVE

The Lucases come to visit the Bennets, and of course the subject of discussion is the ball. In this small, self-contained society, it is inevitable that such an event become the top subject of conversation. All the local gentry were there, and every word that was spoken, every move that was made, were noted and will be commented on.

Mrs. Bennet energetically voices her dislike of Darcy. Charlotte Lucas suggests that with family, fortune—everything—in his favor, Darcy has a *right* to be proud. Elizabeth replies laughingly that she could forgive *his* pride if he had not offended *hers*.

NOTE: This scene gives us our first indication of how different Charlotte and Elizabeth are. Charlotte is sensible and realistic, willing to accept things and people as they are. Elizabeth, for all her jokes, is very idealistic. She has high expectations about life and strict standards of how people should treat each other.

CHAPTER SIX

The ladies of Netherfield and Longbourn have now exchanged visits. Miss Bingley and Mrs. Hurst were cool to Mrs. Bennet and her younger daughters but mentioned that they would like to see more of Jane and Elizabeth. Jane is pleased with their offer of friendship. Elizabeth is not. One thing does please Elizabeth, though: the attention Bingley's sisters are paying to Jane proves that their brother is interested in her. And Elizabeth can tell that Jane is falling in love with Bingley.

The two friends, Elizabeth and Charlotte, talk privately about the effect the newcomers are having on the neighborhood. Elizabeth, always on the lookout for Jane's happiness, mentions to her friend that Jane seems to be falling in love with Bingley but is hiding it well. Elizabeth's view is that a young woman can't let on that she is interested in a man until he openly expresses his interest in her by proposing marriage. If he doesn't, the humiliation of having shown her feelings for him would be too much to bear.

Charlotte disagrees. She thinks Jane is hiding her feelings too well. She makes a shrewd comment: a woman would do well to show a man more than she feels for him, rather than less, in order to encourage him. Elizabeth argues against this point of view. Charlotte is right, she says, *only* if the woman's main purpose is to attract a husband—whether the man loves her or not.

Charlotte makes a startling reply: she says it does not matter how well two people know each other before they marry. Happiness in marriage is entirely a matter of luck, she claims. To her way of thinking, "it is better to know as little as possible of the defects of the person with whom you are to pass your life."

Do you agree with Charlotte? Add her opinion to the growing number of attitudes toward love and marriage—some romantic, some cynical—that *Pride and Prejudice* asks us to consider and evaluate.

NOTE: Charlotte's comments are significant in another way. Her warning that Jane should show her feelings for Bingley gives us a foreshadowing of trouble in that romance. Also, Charlotte's philosophy about marriage gives us a clue to how she will deal with a proposal of marriage that will soon be coming her way.

A major plot development is forecast in this chapter: Darcy is undergoing a change of feeling toward Elizabeth. Having made it clear to his friends that he finds her scarcely pretty, he is now watching her, listening to her conversations with others—he even asks her to dance. She declines, but with such charm that even her rejection pleases him. When Miss Bingley makes a guess that he is thinking of the dullness of the company, he contradicts her. No, he says, he is thinking of "the very great pleasure which a pair of fine eyes in the face of a pretty woman can bestow." To Miss Bingley's astonishment, he even tells her frankly that the woman he means is Elizabeth Bennet. She at once reminds him that Mrs. Bennet would be his mother-in-law if he married Elizabeth. He listens to her mean-spirited comments with indifference. His interest in Elizabeth is established, and so is Miss Bingsley's jealousy.

CHAPTER SEVEN

This chapter begins with a note on property law and social classes. A brief narrative paragraph establishes the facts of Mr. Bennet's moderate income and entailed estate (see Glossary), and of Mrs. Bennet's relatives, who are in trade. Her sister, Mrs. Philips, is the wife of an attorney in Meryton, a mile from Longbourn. The two youngest Bennet girls, Kitty and Lydia, walk to the town almost daily to look in the shops and learn the gossip by visiting to their aunt.

On this day they hear something that to them is great news. A regiment of militia has arrived, to be stationed in the town for the winter. From this moment on, the two girls—especially Lydia—can talk of nothing but the officers and their hopes of being noticed by them.

NOTE: Officers in the military were ranked as gentlemen, whatever the familes of their origin. It was customary for a family to buy a commission in the army or navy for a younger son who could not inherit a title or estate; or they might help out a promising

young man from a lower social class in this way; he
could then make a gentlemanly career in the services.
It would not be out of order for a girl of the Bennet
family to marry an officer, but if neither he nor she
had additional income it would not be wise. They
could not live comfortably on an officer's pay.

Now we get a sample of Mrs. Bennet's plotting.
Jane is invited to dine with Bingley's sisters. The gentlemen are to be away, dining with the officers. Mrs.
Bennet decides that Jane cannot have the carriage but
must go on horseback, because rain threatens. If the
weather turns bad, she will have to stay overnight at
Netherfield, and this will give Bingley's interest in her
an opportunity to ripen.

Mrs. Bennet's scheme works all too well. Jane gets
soaked and is kept in bed at Netherfield with a bad
cold. Elizabeth hurries to her side. Jane feels so ill that
Elizabeth is invited to stay and nurse her.

Here is a new situation, in which the story promises
to take a fresh turn. Jane and Elizabeth are both under
the same roof with Bingley and Darcy. The pace
quickens from here on.

CHAPTER EIGHT

Day and evening follow at Netherfield. Elizabeth
looks after Jane and makes occasional appearances in
the drawing room. Caroline Bingley makes sharp con-
versational jabs at her in her presence and spiteful
comments on her appearance and manners when she
is gone. Bingley disagrees with his sister, but Darcy
keeps quiet. We're not sure at this point whether Caroline is winning him over or not.

CHAPTER NINE

Elizabeth is worried about Jane and sends word to
her mother to come and judge for herself how sick
Jane is. Mrs. Bennet finds Jane in no danger, but sees

no reason to end the visit before her plan to hook Bingley has run its course. She declares that Jane is still too ill to risk the journey home. Bingley agrees: Jane must not take chances, she must stay. Mrs. Bennet and her two youngest daughters stay only a short while, but it is long enough for Elizabeth to be embarrassed by her mother's crude and tactless remarks. Lydia adds to Elizabeth's embarrassment by boldly demanding a promise from Bingley that he will give a ball at Netherfield as soon as Jane is better.

NOTE: Elizabeth can't avoid the realization that her mother and Lydia are social handicaps to both herself and Jane. Mrs. Bennet is too dim-witted to understand Darcy's most casual remark, too self-important to keep from making idiotic answers, and without the social grace to hide her dislike of him. This scene, comic to us as readers, is painful to Elizabeth. She wishes herself a thousand miles away; this is obviously the kind of embarrassment she is doomed to suffer often.

CHAPTER TEN

In the Netherfield drawing room, Elizabeth bends over her needlework, quietly amused by Caroline Bingley's attentions to Darcy, who is writing a letter to his young sister. Caroline just can't hold her tongue. She keeps pouring out compliments and messages for him to tell his sister. He simply goes on writing.

Then follows one of the novel's lively scenes completely constructed in dialogue. The conversation reveals the personalities of Darcy, Bingley, Caroline Bingley, and Elizabeth—and shows Jane Austen at her dramatic best. Wit and repartee flow—and Darcy is so charmed by Elizabeth that he fears falling in love.

CHAPTER ELEVEN

After dinner, Jane, feeling much better, joins the company. Bingley devotes himself entirely to making her comfortable. Darcy takes up a book, and Miss Bingley takes up another. She declares her delight in reading, but in fact she shows more interest in Darcy's progress through his book than in her own. Finally, yawning, she puts her book aside and begins to walk about the room.

Darcy reads on. Miss Bingley invites Elizabeth to join her, and Elizabeth does. At this, to Miss Bingley's annoyance, Darcy at last raises his head to watch.

Conversation resumes. The good-natured teasing between Elizabeth and Darcy becomes so lively that Miss Bingley puts an end to it by going to the piano and beginning to play. Darcy is glad to have his all too obvious interest in Elizabeth interrupted.

CHAPTER TWELVE

Jane and Elizabeth decide it is time to leave Netherfield. Mrs. Bennet, still scheming to keep them there, sends word that she cannot send the Longbourn carriage for them. They ask Bingley for his. He agrees, while expressing his regret at their going. Darcy is troubled at the growing warmth of his feelings toward Elizabeth, so he ignores her during her last day at Netherfield. At home, Mrs. Bennet is angry that her daughters have returned sooner than she planned.

CHAPTER THIRTEEN

The Reverend William Collins, Mr. Bennet's cousin and heir, now enters the story. He writes a letter inviting himself to Longbourn for a two-week stay. Mr.

Bennet is amused by the letter, which goes on and on with explanations, apologies, and self-important remarks.

Mr. Collins arrives. He admires his fair cousins and hints at more than admiration. He praises the house, every room, all the furniture and furnishings piece by piece. Mr. Bennet is entertained. Mrs. Bennet is gratified—until she remembers that what he is admiring will one day be his, when Mr. Bennet dies and the detestable Mr. Collins turns her and her daughters out into the cold. No effort at explanation can make her understand the entail.

NOTE: Mr. Collins's entrance is one of pure comedy. This chapter and the next are two of the funniest in the novel, but notice how Austen also uses these scenes to develop her plot.

CHAPTER FOURTEEN

Mr. Collins regales his cousins with long accounts of his patron and her estate. He boasts of his skill at making compliments that elegant ladies such as Lady Catherine like to hear. Mr. Bennet slyly asks whether he plans these flatteries in advance. Mr. Collins acknowledges that he does, but he takes care not to let them sound artificial. The chapter continues in a comic vein.

CHAPTER FIFTEEN

Mr. Collins reveals that Lady Catherine has urged him to marry. He asks Mrs. Bennet if Jane, the oldest daughter, is available. She tells him that Jane is likely soon to be engaged, and he quickly turns his attentions to Elizabeth. Unsuspecting, Elizabeth is polite to him as she would be to any guest. He accompanies the young ladies on their walk to town.

Here another new character enters the story. The good-looking, charming Mr. Wickham has joined the regiment and is walking with his officer friends. They meet the young ladies from Longbourn. While this is going on, Bingley and Darcy ride up to greet the Bennet party, and Elizabeth witnesses a strange encounter. Darcy and Wickham see each other, both give a start of recognition, but with cold looks and slight nods they barely acknowledge knowing each other.

NOTE: With the introduction of Wickham, the thread of a new subplot begins. The pace of the narrative quickens and suspense is added.

CHAPTER SIXTEEN

During an evening with the officers at Elizabeth's aunt's house, Wickham at once seats himself beside Elizabeth and, without being asked, proceeds to explain the mysterious encounter with Darcy.

It seems he grew up on the Darcy estate as the son of the Darcy steward and the godson of Darcy's late father. Elizabeth admits that she finds Mr. Darcy a disagreeable man, proud and haughty. All the same she is shocked at the story Wickham tells her. According to him, Darcy has refused to give him the "living" he is entitled to—that is, the rectory of the parish in which Darcy's estate is situated. He declares that Darcy has done this even though the position of rector there was bequeathed to him in the elder Darcy's will. Elizabeth is now confronted with the claim that Darcy is not only an unpleasant man but also a dishonorable one.

Wickham further tells her that Mr. Collins's patron, Lady Catherine de Bourgh, is Darcy's aunt and that Darcy is intended to marry her daughter. Thus the plot threads become further intertwined and the narrative gains further suspense.

CHAPTER SEVENTEEN

Elizabeth tells Jane what she has learned from Wickham about Darcy. Jane can't believe it; she is sure there is some misunderstanding. As for Elizabeth, Wickham has won her sympathy; she has only the deepest dislike for Darcy.

Bingley announces the date of the ball he has promised to give at Netherfield. Elizabeth is excited about it and asks Mr. Collins whether, as a clergyman, he disapproves of dancing. On the contrary, says he, and promptly asks her for the first pair of dances. She is dismayed, but must accept. What she is really looking forward to, however, is dancing with Wickham.

CHAPTER EIGHTEEN

Arrived at the ball, Elizabeth looks in vain among the red coats of the officers for Wickham. Did Bingley not invite him out of consideration for Darcy? A fellow officer, however, tells Lydia that Wickham was called to town on business and stayed away an extra day to avoid a certain gentleman. Wickham had told Elizabeth that he had no intention of avoiding Darcy, yet that is just what he is doing.

Elizabeth gets through her dances with the awkward Collins as best she can. Then Darcy asks her to dance, and, too startled to think of an excuse, she accepts. They dance and talk. He is very agreeable, but turns silent the moment she mentions Wickham.

Sir William Lucas, Charlotte's father compliments them both on their dancing. He then refers to a coming desirable event and pointedly looks at Bingley and Jane, who stand talking, their heads close together.

Miss Bingley approaches Elizabeth and rather insolently warns her against taking an interest in Wickham, since he is low-born. She also understands that he has behaved badly to Darcy, although she does not know the details. In softer terms, Bingley has told Jane much the same thing, also by hearsay. Elizabeth judges that since the information comes by way of Mr. Darcy, she need not believe it.

For Elizabeth, the ball offers only increasing unpleasantness. Collins learns that Darcy is present and insists on presenting himself to Lady Catherine's nephew. His pompous speech, punctuated by bow after bow, leaves Darcy somewhat puzzled, but it makes Elizabeth blush with embarrassment. Then at supper Mrs. Bennet talks loudly of her expectation that Jane will soon be engaged to Bingley. Elizabeth sees Darcy across the table, listening. She tries to silence her mother but without success. Darcy looks toward Bingley and Jane, and his face is grave.

CHAPTER NINETEEN

The next day brings a scene of pure comedy. Mr. Collins proposes marriage to Elizabeth, with all the elaborate explanations and compliments that he considers proper to such an occasion. Elizabeth declines politely. He brushes her rejection aside, observing that elegant young ladies are bound to refuse a first proposal, even a second or third. Elizabeth protests that no sensible woman would so mistreat a respectable man or so risk her happiness if she meant to accept him in the end. He does not listen, but persists in his belief that her refusal is ladylike modesty.

CHAPTER TWENTY

Mr. Collins reports in detail to Mrs. Bennet. He repeats that he is not discouraged by Elizabeth's refusal, but will continue to propose to her. Mrs. Bennet, however, knows Elizabeth and she is alarmed. Elizabeth is a headstrong girl, she says. She will command Elizabeth to accept him. Mr. Collins himself is alarmed at her choice of words. A headstrong girl is not the kind of wife he wants.

Charlotte Lucas comes to call as Mrs. Bennet is pouring out her disappointment to Mr. Collins. Mr. Collins withdraws his offer of marriage to Elizabeth once and for all. Charlotte, standing tactfully to one side, hears it all.

CHAPTER TWENTY-ONE

The story begins to move faster. Mr. Collins transfers his attentions to Charlotte, Mr. Wickham renews his attentions to Elizabeth, and Jane receives a good-bye note from Caroline Bingley. Miss Bingley implies that her brother will not return to Netherfield, and she expresses her hope that he will marry Darcy's sister Georgiana.

NOTE: The mood now becomes one of anxiety. Elizabeth tries to raise Jane's spirits with the argument that Miss Bingley is only expressing her own wishes, not her brother's. But privately she fears that Miss Bingley may win out and that Jane's hope of happiness will be dashed.

CHAPTER TWENTY-TWO

Mr. Collins sneaks out to Lucas Lodge and quickly accomplishes his mission. Charlotte is watching for him. As she expects, he makes his proposal of marriage to her. She promptly accepts and instructs him to say nothing to the Bennets of their engagement. He leaves Longbourn, promising to return.

Charlotte confides her news to Elizabeth, who is at first disbelieving, then shocked. She is convinced that her friend can't possibly be happy with this absurd man whom she can't respect, much less love. Charlotte, not offended, answers her. She is not romantic, she says. She asks only for a comfortable home, and considers her chances of happiness as fair as most people's on entering a marriage.

NOTE: Charlotte here expresses an attitude toward marriage that was common among middle-class young women of the time. Security was the main thing, not love. Elizabeth can't accept this philosophy. For her, marriage must be based on mutual affection and respect.

CHAPTER TWENTY-THREE

Sir William Lucas comes to the Bennets' house to announce his daughter's engagement. Mrs. Bennet cannot forgive Elizabeth for losing a husband, but Mr. Bennet is delighted. Lady Lucas can hardly hide her joy at having her plain daughter well married before any of the pretty Bennet girls.

Mr. Collins writes a self-congratulatory letter to Mr. Bennet, reinviting himself for another visit so that he can be close to Charlotte. Mrs. Bennet is furious. Elizabeth has deliberately lost a chance to be married, and with Bingley gone, Jane's prospects do not look as bright as they once seemed. Elizabeth begins to fear that Bingley's sisters may indeed prevail and that Bingley may be gone from Netherfield for good.

CHAPTER TWENTY-FOUR

The mood now definitely changes from comedy to gloom. A letter from Miss Bingley puts an end to Jane's hopes. The Bingleys are settled in London for the winter. Mr. Bingley is an intimate of the Darcy household, where he can pursue his courtship of Georgiana.

Jane is downcast, and Elizabeth is indignant. She is furious at Bingley's sisters, suspects Darcy of conspiring with them, and is angry with Bingley for allowing himself to be influenced against his genuine love for Jane.

With Darcy and his friends gone, Wickham now freely tells his tale to everyone. Darcy is now generally condemned. Elizabeth somehow does not see how improper it is of Wickham to make his story so public. She is still charmed by Wickham and prejudiced against Darcy.

CHAPTER TWENTY-FIVE

The mood again changes as new characters, the Gardiners, enter the story. They come with their children to spend Christmas at Longbourn. Edward Gardiner is Mrs. Bennet's brother, but he is not at all like her or like his other sister, the good-natured but vulgar Mrs. Phillips. He is dignified, gentlemanly, and sensible. His wife, somewhat younger, is both intelligent and elegant, and she is very close to her two oldest nieces. She invites Jane to return with them for a stay in London, pointing out, however, that since they live in an unfashionable quarter of the city it is unlikely she will meet Mr. Bingley.

Mrs. Gardiner meets Wickham. She spent some girlhood years in the neighborhood of the Darcy estate of Pemberley, and she enjoys recalling stories of that part of the country with him. Elizabeth tells her of Darcy's treatment of Wickham, and she tries to remember what she may have heard of Darcy's character. She believes she may have heard of him as a very proud, ill-natured boy.

CHAPTER TWENTY-SIX

In a confidential moment between Elizabeth and her aunt, Mrs. Gardiner cautions Elizabeth against falling in love with Wickham, a man with no fortune. Elizabeth at first laughs off the advice. Then, turning serious, she promises to do her best to be wise.

NOTE: Mrs. Gardiner is the only person Elizabeth has accepted advice from on this subject.

Charlotte comes, after her wedding, to say goodbye. Her father and her younger sister Maria are to visit her in her new home, and she invites Elizabeth to come with them. To the reader this raises interesting possibilities, because Mr. Collins's parsonage is on the edge of Lady Catherine's estate, and Lady Catherine is Mr. Darcy's aunt.

Jane writes from London. She has seen Miss Bingley, and she is at last convinced that Elizabeth is right.

Elizabeth learns that Wickham is interested in a young woman who has just inherited some money, but she excuses this as simple prudence, forgetting that she did not excuse Charlotte's prudence in marrying Mr. Collins. She is still letting her prejudice against Darcy influence her judgment of Wickham.

CHAPTER TWENTY-SEVEN

The setting changes. Elizabeth begins her journey with Sir William and Maria Lucas. On the way to Charlotte's, they stop overnight at the Gardiners' in

London, where Elizabeth finds Jane in poor spirits.

Elizabeth talks with her aunt of Jane's problem. Mrs. Gardiner asks about Wickham's new courtship. Elizabeth exclaims that she is sick of Wickham, Bingley, and Darcy. She is going the next day to see a man without a single agreeable quality (Collins), and she is glad of it.

Before Elizabeth leaves with the Lucases, her aunt invites her to join her and her husband on a summer tour to the Lake District. With this to look forward to, and curious about Charlotte's new home and life, Elizabeth continues the journey into Kent more cheerfully.

CHAPTER TWENTY-EIGHT

At Hunsford parsonage Mr. Collins boasts of his house, his furniture, his gardens, and the splendors of his patron's estate, giving every particular of the size and cost of every item. Charlotte is serene. She hears only what she wishes to hear of her husband's babble. Elizabeth recognizes Charlotte's sensible arrangements of the house and grounds, and she understands how Charlotte has managed to keep her husband busy in the garden or in his study, which faces on the road to Rosings. In this way Charlotte has to endure very little of the company of her husband— who may be entertaining to read about but not to live with.

Miss de Bourgh and her governess drive by, stopping at the parsonage gate. Elizabeth is surprised to see what a pale, thin, sickly-looking girl Mr. Darcy is supposed to be interested in marrying—according to Wickham, that is.

The Collinses and their guests are invited to dine at Rosings the next day.

CHAPTER TWENTY-NINE

Comedy is again the mood as the scene unfolds at
Rosings. The manor house is grand without being
tasteful. Pale, shy little Miss de Bourgh can scarcely
utter a word. Lady Catherine talks steadily in a loud,
aggressive voice. Her questions about Elizabeth's
family, her sisters, their education or lack of it, are just
short of offensive. She criticizes, advises, passes judgment. Elizabeth takes it all in good spirit; she is too
amused to be offended. Lady Catherine is as ridiculous in her way as Mr. Collins is in his. We may won-
der what Darcy thinks of his aunt.

CHAPTER THIRTY

Sir William leaves, and Elizabeth and Maria remain.
Elizabeth enjoys her hours of quiet companionship
with Charlotte and her long, solitary walks in Rosings
park.

The visit is suddenly enlivened by the arrival of
Darcy and his cousin, Colonel Fitzwilliam, who have
come to visit their aunt. With no loss of time, the two
gentlemen call on Charlotte and Elizabeth at the parsonage. Charlotte shrewdly observes that this
promptness is a tribute to Elizabeth. The pace quickens, with a promise of surprises to come.

CHAPTER THIRTY-ONE

The scene is an evening at Rosings. Elizabeth and
Colonel Fitzwilliam engage in lively conversation.
Darcy listens, but Lady Catherine interrupts, wanting
to know what they are talking about and insisting on
being included. This effectively halts the conversation. Elizabeth is asked to play and sing. She does,
and Darcy comes close, charmed by her unaffected
performance. Lady Catherine criticizes Elizabeth's

playing and tells her she should practice more. Elizabeth, watching carefully, can see no evidence that Darcy is interested in little Miss de Bourgh.

NOTE: The reader, of course, knows that Darcy is really interested in Elizabeth, and the way he is now behaving toward her suggests that his interest may soon lead to action.

CHAPTER THIRTY-TWO

Darcy surprises Elizabeth alone when he makes a morning visit to the parsonage. Their conversation is about Bingley's returning or not returning to Netherfield, and it is awkward. Charlotte, finding him there, thinks he must really be in love with Elizabeth. But when she looks for signs, she can't find them. His gaze is often fixed on Elizabeth but it does not seem to be an admiring one. The truth is that Darcy is troubled and doesn't know what to do about his feelings for Elizabeth.

CHAPTER THIRTY-THREE

Darcy persists in his peculiar behavior. He often joins Elizabeth on her walks, but then he seems to have little to say. From Fitzwilliam she learns that Darcy keeps postponing their departure.

Fitzwilliam is clearly attracted to her, but he explains, somewhat in apology, that a younger son cannot marry whom he chooses. (He has to find a wife with more money than Elizabeth has.)

She mentions Darcy's sister, and Fitzwilliam tells her that he shares the guardianship of Georgiana with Darcy. She asks an idle question about whether the young girl gives her guardians much trouble. To her surprise, this evokes an anxious response from him.

Had Elizabeth heard any rumor of the kind? No, says Elizabeth, but his reaction suggests that her chance reference to trouble may have come close to the truth.

Then Fitzwilliam unwittingly tells Elizabeth something she is not supposed to know. He says that Darcy recently saved a friend from an unwise attachment. There was no criticism of the young lady, he understands, only of her family.

Elizabeth is sure that the friend he refers to is Bingley, the young lady is Jane, and the family is her own. Her suspicion has been confirmed: Darcy deliberately came between Bingley and Jane. Her anger rises. Back in the parsonage, she bursts into tears, and this brings on a headache. The last person she wishes to see is Darcy, and she has been invited to tea at Rosings. She claims to be ill and begs to be excused.

NOTE: At this point all comedy has now been put aside. The story has taken a dramatic turn.

CHAPTER THIRTY-FOUR

It is evening, the Collinses have gone to Rosings, and Elizabeth is alone. She is rereading all of Jane's letters, looking for—and finding—evidence that Jane is unhappy. She is growing more and more angry, when suddenly Darcy, the object of her anger, walks in. He has presumably come to learn if she is feeling better. He asks, she answers, and he begins to walk restlessly around the room. Finally he comes to a halt and bursts out: "In vain have I struggled. It will not do. My feelings will not be repressed. You must allow me to tell you how ardently I admire and love you."

Elizabeth is too shocked to speak. Taking this as encouragement, he goes on to tell her all the reasons why he should not have made this proposal. He gives her a most unloverlike description of her family and the inferiority of her social standing as compared with his own. His pride is showing.

Elizabeth is now indignant. What angers her above all is his obvious confidence that she will not refuse him. Now it is his turn to be taken aback: she rejects him. She tells him that even if she did not positively dislike him, she would not marry him, and she gives her reasons. Her first is that he has deliberately ruined the happiness of her beloved sister by separating Bingley from her. Her second is that he cruelly deprived Wickham of the secure future that the elder Mr. Darcy had planned for him.

She ends by telling him that there was no way he could have proposed to her that would have persuaded her to accept him. From the beginning of their acquaintance, his arrogance, conceit, and disregard for the feelings of others have convinced her that he was the last man in the world she could ever marry.

Astonished and mortified, Darcy wishes her health and happiness and leaves the house.

NOTE: In this scene the antagonism of Darcy's pride and Elizabeth's prejudice reaches its climax. It is a scene to note, not only for the strong feelings it brings to the surface, but for its dramatic form. It has been transferred to stage and screen with almost no change. The two leading characters stand face to face, hiding nothing, speaking their true feelings about each other.

Darcy has revealed not only his love but all his objections to a marriage to Elizabeth, yet he is certain that she will accept him. Elizabeth is surprised by his offer, although we have been warned of his feelings toward her. She is flattered by a proposal from a man of his position, but at the same time insulted by his references to her family and her inferior social position, and outraged by his obvious confidence that she will not refuse him. And so, instead of expressing gratitude for his love and regret at causing him pain, she rejects him with all the strongest words at her command.

Both characters speak out of powerful feelings here. Some critics complain that Jane Austen never gets to the hearts of her characters. You might use this scene as evidence to the contrary.

Now the reader is truly in suspense. How can the bitter confrontation between these two leading characters be resolved? Will Darcy continue to be in love with Elizabeth when she has made it so clear that she detests him? And if he continues to love her, how can he ever overcome her antagonism toward him? What defense can he offer for the behavior that she has so severely criticized? What can he possibly have to say for himself?

CHAPTER THIRTY-FIVE

We learn the answers to some of these questions in the very next chapter. Darcy waits for Elizabeth on her morning walk, hands her a letter, and asks her to do him the honor of reading it. She begins to read it without believing a word of it. But as she goes back over it again and again, her attitude toward its contents begins to change.

Darcy has answered her two angry accusations of the evening before. To the first, he admits that he persuaded Bingley not to pursue his courtship of

Jane. He admits also that he concealed Jane's presence in London from Bingley, a deception of which he is somewhat ashamed. But he justifies his interference on the grounds that it could not have been a good marriage, considering the behavior of the younger Bennet girls, their mother, and even their father. He declares that, before he intervened, he watched Jane carefully, and from the untroubled serenity of her behavior he became convinced that she did not return Bingley's love at all. If he was mistaken, and if he has indeed caused pain to her, he apologizes. He acted from the best of his knowledge and observation.

To Elizabeth's second accusation, about his treatment of Wickham, Darcy turns Wickham's story completely around. He tells Elizabeth that Wickham gave up all interest in a church career and asked Darcy instead for a sizable sum of money, with the intention of studying law. Darcy gave him what he asked (the sum was £3,000) but instead of beginning studies, Wickham squandered the money on idleness and gambling. In debt again, as a last resort he approached Georgiana. Trading on childhood affection, Wickham persuaded Georgiana to elope with him. Fortunately Georgiana, a loving and dutiful sister, confessed the plan to her brother in time to halt it.

Darcy tells Elizabeth that he trusts her with these painful facts, which could be damaging to his sister's reputation, knowing that he can rely on her to keep them confidential. He also tells her that she can verify the story with Colonel Fitzwilliam, who as his fellow guardian is acquainted with it all. He ends his letter with a generous "God bless you."

Here are several points for Elizabeth to ponder. One is the confirmation that Darcy did in fact steer Bingley away from Jane. A second is that he did not do this unfeelingly, but took the possibility of causing pain to Jane into consideration. Elizabeth remembers what Charlotte once said—that Jane might be concealing her love for Bingley all too well.

Next is the revelation of Wickham's true character. He stands forth in this account as an idler, a gambler, an irresponsible, dissipated man who will go so far as to lead a young girl astray, just to get his hands on her fortune—although in this case, as Darcy suggested, Wickham might also have wanted to take revenge on Darcy by harming his sister.

Darcy, on the other hand, appears totally innocent.

NOTE: Is Darcy's version the truth? What will Elizabeth believe? How will she feel toward Darcy now? Toward Wickham? In addition to these suspenseful questions, we have also received a warning: Watch out for Wickham as a possible source of trouble.

CHAPTER THIRTY-SIX

We follow Elizabeth's reactions to Darcy's letter. At first she is angry and disbelieving. After all, she thinks, Darcy has expressed no regret at destroying Jane's happiness—he is still proud and insolent. And in his story of Wickham, she is certain he is lying from start to finish. She will pay no attention to the letter. She puts it away, resolving never to look at it again.

In the next moment she is reading it a second time. Now she is struck by certain truths. For instance, all along she has known nothing about Wickham except what he himself told her. She has accepted his charm and good looks as evidence of his good character.

Now, for the first time, she realizes how improper it was for him to confide in her, a perfect stranger, on their first meeting. She recalls that he spread his story through the town the moment the Bingleys and Darcy had left the neighborhood. She begins to feel ashamed of her blind acceptance of Wickham and her unreasoning prejudice against Darcy. She decides that although Darcy has told her to consult Colonel Fitzwilliam for the truth of all this, it would be awkward to ask him and surely it is unnecessary.

She returns once more to his comments about Bingley and Jane. She acknowledges now that Jane did indeed conceal her feelings too well, and Darcy could not be blamed for mistaking them. She remembers how her mother embarrassed her at the Netherfield ball, and she feels the justice of Darcy's comments about her family. Then she feels, with something like despair, that Jane's loss of love and happiness can be blamed on her own family.

After hours of walking and thinking, Elizabeth returns to the parsonage and learns that both Darcy and Fitzwilliam have called to say goodbye. She is glad that she missed them, since she is no longer interested in Colonel Fitzwilliam, and her feelings towards Darcy are in complete confusion.

NOTE: This chapter is the beginning of Elizabeth's exploration of her own mind and emotions. Her earnest self-examination is one of the strengths of the novel.

CHAPTER THIRTY-SEVEN

Now that the two gentlemen have left, Elizabeth speaks of her own and Maria's imminent departure. The mood shifts back to comedy briefly, as Lady

Catherine lays down all the details for the coming journey, including how the trunks should be packed. Maria is so intimidated that on returning to the parsonage she takes all her clothes out again and repacks them according to Lady Catherine's advice.

But the story soon turns back to Elizabeth's serious thoughts. She spends her remaining mornings in solitary walks, sorting out her confusing emotions.

She arrives at some certainties. For one thing, she believes now that Bingley's affection for Jane was not just a passing infatuation but deep and sincere, and she can criticize him only for trusting too completely to another's judgment.

She admits to herself that her family has some serious defects. She loves and admires her father, but she knows that he is wrong to be merely amused at his wife and younger daughters; he should instead take the trouble to control them.

She is ashamed of her attack on Darcy. But she cannot honestly admit any regret at having refused him, and she feels no desire to see him again. For now, she feels only worry for Jane, disappointment in Wickham, and a lack of hope that anything can change for the better for either Jane or herself.

CHAPTER THIRTY-EIGHT

It is the day of departure. Mr. Collins makes his farewells in his excessive, exaggerated style. When Elizabeth does not praise his house, his gardens, his marriage, and his patron's attentions eloquently enough, he does the job himself. He also boasts of the success of his marriage. In his eyes, he and Charlotte are in total agreement about everything.

If Elizabeth were not so concerned with her own troubles, she would find his illusion laughable. She doubts Charlotte's happiness, but she admits to herself that her friend at least seems contented with her domestic concerns.

At the Gardiners', she finds Jane feeling better. She keeps all mention of Darcy and the surprising turn of events at Hunsford for when she and Jane are home again at Longbourn.

CHAPTER THIRTY-NINE

Lydia and Kitty meet their sisters with the Bennet carriage at an inn on the road home. Lydia, giddy as usual, rattles on about a new bonnet, about the regiment's plans to leave Meryton, and about the fact that Wickham is no longer pursuing the young heiress—whose family has sent her out of his reach to relations in Liverpool.

At home, Lydia still chatters on about the officers. Mrs. Bennet talks about persuading Mr. Bennet to send them all to Brighton, the seaside resort where the militia will be encamped for the summer. Elizabeth is relieved that her father has no intention of doing so. But because he gives only a vague answer, Mrs. Bennet is not discouraged.

NOTE: The follies of Elizabeth's family now seem poignant instead of comic—to Elizabeth, and to the reader.

CHAPTER FORTY

Elizabeth at last unburdens herself to Jane, being careful to tell her sister only about Darcy and Wickham. She doesn't mention anything about Bingley—and Darcy's influence over him.

Elizabeth makes her story of Darcy's proposal and his letter of the next day as cheerful and entertaining as she can. Jane is grieved for both Darcy and Wickham. Elizabeth teases her: "There is but such a quantity of merit between them; just enough to make one good sort of man; and of late it has been shifting about pretty much. For my part, I am inclined to believe it all Mr. Darcy's; but you shall do as you choose." She says, too, that there was some great mistake in the case of those two young men: "One has got all the goodness, and the other all the appearance of it."

Elizabeth is able, too, to laugh at herself: she meant to be uncommonly clever in taking so strong a dislike to Darcy, she says, but her behavior turned out to be "such a spur to one's genius, such an opening for wit."

Turning serious, she asks Jane's opinion on whether they should expose Wickham's true character to their friends. Jane agrees with her that there is no need, as Wickham will soon be gone with the regiment. As you will see, this turns out to be an unwise decision.

CHAPTER FORTY-ONE

Mrs. Bennet joins Lydia in bemoaning the departure of the militia. She cannot understand why Mr. Bennet will not let the family go to Brighton. Then, unexpectedly, a colonel's young wife invites Lydia to accompany her. Lydia is delighted, Kitty devastated.

Elizabeth protests to her father against letting Lydia go. She tells him that Lydia's uncontrolled behavior will eventually lead to her disgrace and that the misfortune will involve the entire family, including herself and Jane.

Mr. Bennet sees that she is serious, and he reassures her that she and Jane will be valued wherever they are known. But he is really considering his own convenience rather than his family's welfare. He tells Elizabeth that there will be no peace at Longbourn if Lydia is prevented from going, and that at Brighton she will go unnoticed among so many women attractive to the officers.

The officers, including Wickham, are invited to dine at Longbourn before they leave. At this last meeting with him, Elizabeth answers his questions about Hunsford, then tells him of seeing Darcy there—pointedly enough to make him uneasy abut what she may have learned. He covers his embarrassment by talking of Darcy's expectation of marrying Miss de Bourgh. Elizabeth is amused. She knows better.

CHAPTER FORTY-TWO

NOTE: Darcy's letter criticized not only Elizabeth's mother and younger sisters, but her father as well. Although she is her father's favorite and very close to him, Elizabeth also sees his failures—with his younger daughters and with his wife. In this chapter the mood changes to a serious look at the quality of the Bennets' marriage and the relationship of husband and wife.

Mr. Bennet does not behave properly toward his wife. As a girl she had all the charms of youth and beauty to win him, but her ignorance and shallowness soon cooled his affection and respect. He has not consoled himself for the failure of his marriage by drinking, gambling, or pursuing other pleasures—as some men might. But he does indulge himself in ridiculing his wife—in front of their daughters. For a husband to behave in this disrespectful way to his wife encourages her children also to lose respect for their mother. To Elizabeth, this is the wrong way for a husband and father to behave. Her parents are not an example of a happy marriage.

Now Elizabeth's worry about Lydia at Brighton, combined with Mrs. Bennet's and Kitty's complaints about not being there too, make for great unpleasantness at home. Elizabeth begins to look forward to her promised summer tour with the Gardiners, which has been postponed and will also be shorter than planned. They will not have time to go to the Lakes but only as far as Derbyshire.

At this point Elizabeth cannot help thinking of Pemberley, Darcy's estate in Derbyshire—and even of Darcy himself. She laughs at herself for these thoughts. Surely she can set foot in his county without his noticing her! This raises the question of whether she wants him to notice her.

NOTE: Not long ago Elizabeth was sure she never cared to see Darcy again. Now her feelings seem to be changing.

At last the Gardiners arrive, place their four young children in Jane's care, and set off with Elizabeth in their carriage. Soon they come to Lambton, the town Mrs. Gardiner remembers from her girlhood. Pemberley is only five miles away, and Mrs. Gardiner wants to revisit it. A nervous Elizabeth makes excuses not to go there, until she learns from the chambermaid that the Darcy family is away. With the danger of meeting Darcy removed, she agrees to go.

CHAPTER FORTY-THREE

Driving through the extensive Pemberley grounds to the handsome house, Elizabeth finds everything beautiful. She reflects that she might now have been mistress of all this. But then she remembers that her beloved uncle and aunt could not have been with her here. Darcy would consider them "inferior."

As was the custom at great houses in England, the travelers are welcomed, and the housekeeper gives them a tour of the house. Elizabeth hears with relief that Darcy is not expected until the following day. Relaxing, she looks at the fine rooms, the views, the furniture, and the pleasing decorations.

On learning that Elizabeth knows Darcy "a little," the housekeeper begins to praise him—his handsomeness, his good temper, his goodness to his sister, his generosity to his servants and tenants. She has known him, she says, since he was four years old and has never heard a cross word from him.

Elizabeth is shaken by this. She stands before his portrait in the family picture gallery. His face in the painting wears a smile that she has seen only sometimes when he was looking at her. Elizabeth's feelings toward him are changing. She is forgetting her anger at him and remembering only his love for her. She feels, for the first time, grateful for that love.

The mood of this chapter has been suspenseful, and now suddenly the suspense comes to a head. The visitors have left the house and are about to be shown through the grounds when Darcy suddenly appears around the corner of the house from the stables, where he has evidently just dismounted from his horse.

He and Elizabeth both stop, startled at this unexpected meeting. He astonishes her by coming to greet her. He asks after her family and speaks with a gentleness she has never heard from him before.

He leaves her, and she and the Gardiners begin their walk. But in a few minutes Darcy again appears. He asks to be introduced to the Gardiners, whom Elizabeth had expected him to scorn. He joins her uncle in conversation, invites him to fish in the Pemberley trout stream while he is in the neighborhood, and even offers to supply him with fishing tackle.

To Elizabeth, who is still embarrassed at his finding her there, he explains that he has indeed come home a day before he was expected. He tells her that the Bingleys will be coming the next day and that his sister will be with them. He asks Elizabeth's permission to introduce his sister to her, an extraordinary compliment. The walk, uneasy for them both, comes to an end. Darcy helps the ladies into their carriage and then departs with utmost politeness.

On the way back to their inn, her uncle and aunt comment on their pleasant impression of Darcy, whom Elizabeth had formerly described as so disagreeable. She answers that she has never seen him so pleasant before. She also hints that she has reliable information about his treatment of Wickham, different from what she had before. Inwardly, Elizabeth is amazed. Darcy clearly holds no grudge from their last meeting. She can think of nothing but his changed behavior to her, and she wonders what it means.

CHAPTER FORTY-FOUR

Darcy brings his sister to call the very morning of her arrival at Pemberley. Bingley arrives soon after. The Gardiners are beginning to suspect that Darcy is in love with Elizabeth: that is the only thing that can account for his attentiveness.

Bingley asks after Elizabeth's family. Elizabeth listens closely for signs that he is still thinking of Jane. She hears such a clue when he remembers the exact date on which he last saw the Bennets.

Elizabeth finds the young Miss Darcy to be shy rather than proud; she is also unsure of her social duties. Darcy has to remind her that she wishes to invite the visitors to dinner at Pemberly the next day.

The visit leaves Elizabeth more confused than ever about her own feelings.

NOTE: In this and succeeding chapters, Elizabeth continues her self-examination. It is a powerful factor in keeping up the suspense of the story at this crucial stage. As Darcy reveals more and more of the softer aspects of his personality, Elizabeth must respond to her changing image of him. Her feelings, along with her understanding, are now continually shifting.

Mrs. Gardiner is full of curiosity about the relationship of Elizabeth and Darcy but too tactful to ask Elizabeth. Instead she casually inquires among her friends in the town about his reputation among them. They have little to say about him except that he is believed to be proud, a predictable opinion from townsfolk about the wealthy, aloof aristocrat in their neighborhood. They know more of Wickham, and their judgment is not favorable. He left the neighborhood owing many debts, which, they tell her, Darcy paid.

CHAPTER FORTY-FIVE

Elizabeth and the Gardiners pay their morning call at Pemberley, Mr. Gardiner to fish, the ladies to return the visit of the day before. Bingley's sisters are barely civil, and Georgiana is too shy to talk.

Darcy comes in from the fishing party to greet the guests, and Caroline Bingley at once makes a nasty reference to the militia leaving the Bennets' neighborhood. Elizabeth notes Georgiana's distress at this indirect reference to Wickham. As for Darcy, he is looking earnestly at Elizabeth, wondering how she now feels about Wickham—and about himself.

After Elizabeth and Mrs. Gardiner leave, Caroline Bingley exclaims that Elizabeth has become "so coarse and brown." Darcy answers mildly that this is a natural consequence of traveling in the summer. Caroline, driven by jealousy, reminds him that he once thought Elizabeth pretty. His answer can hardly please her. That was only when he first knew Elizabeth, he says, but now he considers her "one of the handsomest women of my acquaintance."

NOTE: We are not kept in any doubt about Darcy's continuing love for Elizabeth. The crucial question is: will he again attempt to make her an offer of marriage? Elizabeth is beginning to ask herself the same question. She is less and less certain of what her own answer, this time, might be.

CHAPTER FORTY-SIX

Two hastily written letters from Jane at Longbourn upset all hopes and speculations. The news brings disgrace on the entire family: Lydia has run away with Wickham. At first it was thought that they were going to Scotland, where marriage can take place without the delays imposed in England. It now appears that they have gone into hiding in London. Wickham is now known to his fellow officers as a man not to be trusted, and his colonel thinks it unlikely that he means to marry Lydia. A troubled Mr. Bennet has gone to London to try to find the fugitives. In the letter Jane begs her uncle to join her father in London as soon as possible and bring his better judgment to the situation.

Elizabeth is hurrying out to find her uncle in the town when Darcy comes in to pay a morning call. He is shocked at her pale face and anxious manner, believing she is ill. He sends a servant to find her aunt and uncle, and begs her to let him get her a glass of wine. She protests that she is not ill, and in her agitation, moved by his concern, she blurts out all her dreadful news. She blames herself for not preventing the disaster by telling what she knew of Wickham's true character.

Darcy is at first concerned only for her distress, but then he begins to walk around the room, seemingly inattentive, grave and thoughtful. At last he hastily excuses himself and leaves her. As soon as he is gone, Elizabeth feels the full weight of this horrid turn of events as it affects her. With this scandal, which must stain the entire Bennet family, Darcy's interest in her must surely melt away.

His preoccupation, during the last few minutes of his visit, seems proof to Elizabeth that this process has already begun: whatever love he still feels for her must be cooling. Now, when all hope of having his love seems lost, Elizabeth realizes how much she wishes that he still loved her.

The Gardiners return, and Elizabeth tells them the news. They pack quickly and leave at once for Longbourn. As they hurry away, Mrs. Gardiner reminds Elizabeth that they have a dinner engagement at Pemberley that must be broken. But Elizabeth has already made their excuses to Darcy, and she tells her aunt, "*That* is all settled!"

"*What* is all settled?" wonders Mrs. Gardiner, baffled by Elizabeth's uncommunicative behavior. But Elizabeth herself would not be able to say at this point what is or is not settled, except that she can now see no hope that Darcy will ever interest himself in her again.

CHAPTER FORTY-SEVEN

The journey back to Longbourn is occupied with speculation on whether Wickham did or did not intend to marry Lydia and make their elopement

respectable. The Gardiners can hardly believe that he
is wicked enough to seduce a girl of good family and
then abandon her, or foolish enough to expect that he
would be allowed to get away with it. Elizabeth now
tells them that he is indeed capable of all that. She tells
them what she now knows of Wickham, but she does
not tell them how and from whom she learned the
truth. Hopeless as she now feels about her own prospects, she cannot bring herself to tell them about Darcy's proposal to her, her refusal, and his extraordinary
letter that reversed all her previous beliefs about Wickham and himself.

They arrive at Longbourn. Mr. Bennet has written
from London but without news of the fugitives. Mrs.
Bennet has taken to her bed in this crisis. She weeps,
complains of her nerves, and begs her brother to keep
Mr. Bennet from fighting a duel with Wickham and
getting himself killed. In the same breath she instructs
him to tell Lydia not to order her wedding trousseau
without consulting her.

Consulting with Jane, Elizabeth learns that Wickham left debts and bad feeling all over Meryton when
the militia went away. She again regrets that she did
not tell their friends and neighbors what she knew of
him. Jane shows her the letter Lydia left for her host-
ess at Brighton. It raves about her dear Wickham and
says what a joke it will be when she writes to her
family and surprises them by signing her letter "Mrs.
Wickham." Thoughtless and careless of consequences
as Lydia might be, the letter indicates that she at least
expected to be married.

CHAPTER FORTY-EIGHT

Mr. Gardiner writes from London. The fugitives
have still not been traced. Perhaps, he says, Elizabeth
can say whether Wickham had family or friends from

whom more might be learned. Elizabeth is embarrassed: she remembers her former partiality toward Wickham, which has prompted her uncle's inquiry.

Aunt Phillips from Meryton comes with further news of Wickham's wicked reputation in the town. Meanwhile, the scandal has, of course, reached to Hunsford, and a letter arrives from Mr. Collins. It is typical of Collins—a confused mixture of condolence, advice, and horrified respectability. He quotes Lady Catherine, who points out the inevitable damage to the older daughters' prospects. Mr. Collins closes with the conflicting advice that the family forgive Lydia and at the same time throw her out to reap the fruits of her offense.

Mr. Bennet returns home, leaving the search for Lydia and Wickham to Gardiner. Now Mrs. Bennet, reversing herself, complains that her husband will not, after all, fight a duel with Wickham. Thus, in the midst of crisis, we are given comedy. Mr. Collins and Mrs. Bennet are still called upon to make us laugh.

NOTE: The comic touches in this chapter are a clue that the story may still have a happy ending.

CHAPTER FORTY-NINE

An express (special delivery) letter arrives from Mr. Gardiner. The fugitives have been found and he has seen them. Wickham's circumstances are not hopeless: his debts will be paid, and there will be some money left over as a marriage settlement for Lydia. They will be married as soon as Mr. Bennet agrees to make a small annual allowance to Lydia out of her mother's dowry. In the meantime she is to stay with the Gardiners, and she will be married from their house.

Mr. Bennet's reaction to this good news is in character: he makes a joke about it. As he is walking in the garden, putting off the unpleasant task of answering the letter, he thinks about how little is being asked of him. He is to promise a hundred pounds a year to Lydia during his lifetime and fifty pounds after his death. He says that Wickham is a fool to marry Lydia for so little: "I should be sorry to think so ill of him, in the very beginning of our relationship."

Elizabeth ponders the fact that they must be happy about this marriage even though it can bring very little happiness to the partners and is necessary only to give the pair some respectability. She and Jane worry that their uncle must have spent a great deal to pay Wickham's debts and still have something left over for Lydia's marriage settlement (her dowry).

They hurry to their mother's room to tell her the news. She is beside herself with joy. She seems to forget the unfortunate circumstances and is simply thrilled that she is to have a daughter married, and at sixteen! She chatters on about Lydia's trousseau, and wants Jane to ask Mr. Bennet how much he will give for it. Jane reminds her mother that her brother has laid out a considerable sum—they do not know how much—just to bring about this happy event. They are hardly in the financial position to start planning a trousseau. Mrs. Bennet is unfazed by Jane's realistic assessment of the situation. She calls her housekeeper to help her dress so that she can spread the good news of Lydia's wedding in town.

NOTE: The comic aspects of this chapter provide entertainment and keep the novel from rushing too swiftly to its resolution. The reactions of Mr. and Mrs. Bennet to the crisis and its resolution also further define their characters.

CHAPTER FIFTY

In a thoughtful mood Mr. Bennet thinks about the money his brother-in-law has laid out to bring about this marriage of his daughter to one of the most worthless young men in Great Britain—a great irony. At the same time, he worries about how he can ever repay Edward Gardiner. He has never saved any part of his income, expecting always to have a son who would inherit his estate and keep it in the family.

He ponders on how little trouble Lydia's rescue has caused him. It has been accomplished with no exertion on his part and little expense. He is obliged only to give her now the share she would eventually have been entitled to anyway out of her mother's modest fortune: the hundred pounds a year is only slightly more than Lydia's clothes and pocket money have cost him until now.

Mrs. Bennet runs down the list of all the fine houses she knows in the neighborhood and considers which would be grand enough for her newly married daughter. She is shocked when Mr. Bennet says he will give Lydia no money for wedding clothes and will not receive the newlyweds in his house.

Another letter from Mr. Gardiner tells the family that Wickham is leaving the militia, and that a commission has been bought for him in the regular army. The couple will go from London to his regiment, stationed in Newcastle in the north. Jane and Elizabeth persuade their father to change his mind and receive them before they leave.

Elizabeth thinks how happy Darcy would be to know that his offer of marriage, which she spurned so fiercely, would now be welcome. She has already come to the sad conclusion, however, that with Wickham in the family there is no possibility that Darcy will renew his offer. He could never marry someone who is related to Wickham: no kind of pride, she believes, would accept that.

NOTE: In this chapter we see not only the evolution of Elizabeth's feelings but also the evolution of the novel's concept of pride. In the beginning of the novel, pride was synonymous with arrogance, insolence, and conceit. Then it was seen as a recognition of one's own superior status in terms of family and fortune. Now Elizabeth sees it as a judgment of social behavior: no one with any pride would accept Wickham. Remember, though, that Wickham himself said earlier that Darcy's pride led him into good behavior on occasion. Soon to be revealed, as Darcy's latest acts become known, is an interpretation of pride as a taking of responsibility.

CHAPTER FIFTY-ONE

The newly married pair arrive. Lydia is her exuberant, uncontrolled self. She shows off her wedding ring. She boasts that she will get all her sisters husbands when they visit her: an army encampment is the very place for finding husbands, she says. Wickham is also his usual smiling, socially agreeable self. He shows no more embarrassment than Lydia does in front of the family, no shame over their affair before they were married. He sits beside Elizabeth, casually chatting about mutual acquaintances in the neighborhood.

Elizabeth sees that, as she had imagined, Lydia is far more attached to Wickham than he is to her, and that he fled from Brighton to escape his debts, not out of love for Lydia. The elopement can be explained by two circumstances: his financial distress and Lydia's infatuation.

Lydia boisterously recounts for Jane and Elizabeth the details of her wedding. She was annoyed by aunt Gardiner's preaching, and by the fact that she wasn't allowed to leave the house for parties or anything before the wedding. She was worried when uncle Gardiner, who was to give her away, was called away to business just before they were to go to the church. But then she remembered that Darcy would do just as well. "Darcy!" her sisters exclaim. Oh yes, he was to bring Wickham to the church. But it was a secret. No one was supposed to know about Darcy.

In that case, says Jane, Lydia must say nothing more. But Elizabeth has to know the rest. She sits down at once and writes to her aunt, begging to know what Darcy had to do with the event.

CHAPTER FIFTY-TWO

Mrs. Gardiner answers promptly and fully: Darcy, knowing something of Wickham's past associations, was able to trace the couple. After he found them, he sought out Mr. Gardiner and informed him of what he had accomplished: he had paid Wickham's debts, paid Lydia's dowry, and bought Wickham his army commission. In return he got Wickham to agree to the marriage. All this, says Mrs. Gardiner, he insisted on doing himself. She surmises that obstinacy may be, after all, the chief defect in his character. The reason he gave for taking all this responsibility upon himself was that he held himself to blame for keeping Wickham's true character a secret from the world in general.

Elizabeth is sitting in the garden, thinking over all this, her mind in a flutter, when Wickham joins her. He mentions that he passed Darcy several times in

London and wondered what he was doing there. To this outright lie Elizabeth does not respond. He asks her about her visit to Pemberley. From her careful answers he finally realizes that his lies are useless: she now knows the truth about him. She tells him that they need not quarrel about the past.

Elizabeth now has a new trouble on her mind: her family owes so much to Darcy, and she is unable to thank him for it. She can hardly even hope she will ever see him again.

CHAPTER FIFTY-THREE

News comes that Bingley is returning to Netherfield. Mrs. Bennet rattles on about it, protesting that of course it is nothing to her and yet insisting on talking about nothing else. Jane is clearly uneasy, but she tells Elizabeth she no longer has any interest in Bingley.

Bingley arrives at Netherfield. Very soon afterwards, he comes to call on the Bennets, and Darcy is with him. Elizabeth struggles to stay calm when she first sees him. He asks about the Gardiners, then is silent.

Mrs. Bennet chatters on about Lydia's marriage to Wickham, and Elizabeth is overcome with embarrassment, knowing what she does of Darcy's role in Lydia's rescue. She wishes at that moment that she never had to see him again, never had to live through another such scene. In the next moment she forgets her own misery, though—seeing how warmly attentive Bingley is to Jane. Mrs. Bennet invites both men to dinner, and they accept.

It is clear to Elizabeth that Darcy has changed his mind about Bingley's courtship of Jane. But what of Darcy, and his interest in Elizabeth? If he still cares for her, why his silence? Has Darcy come calling merely to make certain of his friend's happiness? Or has he come on his own account, to see her?

CHAPTER FIFTY-FOUR

Elizabeth is annoyed at Darcy's silence, but amused at Jane's insistence that she and Bingley are now no more than acquaintances.

The two gentlemen arrive for dinner. They are part of a large party. Bingley "happens" to sit next to Jane, but Darcy is seated beside Mrs. Bennet. Elizabeth trembles at her thoughts of their conversation. It seems to her that everything that went wrong before is going wrong again.

She hopes that after dinner Darcy will come over to her. She is pouring the coffee, and he approaches, but as he does a little girl comes up to Elizabeth and whispers to her; Darcy turns away. In the next moment Mrs. Bennet captures him again, and Elizabeth's evening comes to nothing. But Jane, still professing friendly calm toward Bingley, is glowing with happiness.

CHAPTER FIFTY-FIVE

Bingley keeps coming to Longbourn, and now Mrs. Bennet begins scheming to leave him alone with Jane. She calls Kitty, then Elizabeth, out of the room. By one device and another, Bingley at last finds the opportunity to make his proposal to Jane and to ask her father for his consent. Mrs. Bennet is wild with joy: a second daughter about to be married!

Jane is radiant. She confides to Elizabeth that when Bingley left Netherfield last November, he was truly in love with her, but he had been persuaded that she did not return his love. Elizabeth silently commends Bingley for not betraying his friend's part in the matter.

NOTE: Elizabeth's state of suspense tells us that the story may still have some surprises for us.

CHAPTER FIFTY-SIX

One of these surprises now occurs: Lady Catherine de Bourgh comes to call. Elizabeth is puzzled. She brings no letter or message from Charlotte Collins. Why has she come all the way from Kent and left her personal maid in the coach waiting for her? Lady Catherine asks Elizabeth to go out in the garden with her and at once comes to the point: Elizabeth must promise not to marry Darcy!

In a scene of high comedy, Lady Catherine marshals all her arguments: that years ago she and Darcy's late mother agreed that her daughter and Darcy would marry; that Elizabeth would be scorned by all of Darcy's connections, and especially by Lady Catherine herself; that Elizabeth is an obstinate, headstrong girl who shows no gratitude for Lady Catherine's attentions to her when she was at Hunsford; and so on.

Elizabeth answers only when an answer is demanded of her. When Lady Catherine demands to know whether her nephew has proposed to Elizabeth, Elizabeth reminds her that her ladyship has already declared that to be impossible. When asked if she is engaged to Darcy, she answers truthfully that she is not. But she will make no promises. Lady Catherine demands that she promise, and says she will not leave until Elizabeth does.

She reminds Elizabeth that the Bennet family has low-class connections. Elizabeth responds that Darcy is a gentleman and she is a gentleman's daughter, and therefore they are social equals. Lady Catherine acknowledges this, but what of her mother's relatives

that are "in trade"? And what of her sister's elopement, her patched-up marriage? Is the son of Darcy's
father's late steward to be Darcy's brother-in-law?
"Are the shades of Pemberley to be thus polluted?"

At this, Elizabeth is angered at last. She tells Lady
Catherine that she has now been insulted in every
possible way. Then she goes into the house, with
Lady Catherine's parting threat still in her ears: "I
shall now know how to act. . . . Depend upon it, I
shall carry my point."

NOTE: Lady Catherine's threat can't be ignored
entirely; we don't yet know what influence she has
over Darcy.

CHAPTER FIFTY-SEVEN

Elizabeth is uneasy over Lady Catherine's visit,
ridiculous though it was. She speculates that the news
of Jane's engagement to Bingley, traveling swiftly
from Lucas Lodge to Hunsford parsonage to Rosings,
must have given rise to the assumption that Elizabeth
would become engaged to Bingley's friend.

Elizabeth has no doubt that Lady Catherine means
to persist in her interference. The question is how
much influence she has over Darcy. How fond is he of
his aunt? How much does he depend on her judgment? He must have a higher opinion of Lady Catherine than Elizabeth has, and the very arguments that
to her seemed ridiculous might have far more force
with him, she reasons.

Elizabeth knows that Darcy wavered before first
proposing to her. With his aunt loudly restating all the
reasons why he shouldn't marry into the Bennet family, won't he choose to preserve his dignity at the
expense of his love? Elizabeth decides that if Darcy

sends some excuse instead of returning to Nether-field, she will take that as a sign. She will give up all expectations, and soon she will even stop regretting that she lost him—or so she tells herself.

Her father summons her to his study. He says he has something to show her that will surely amuse her, a letter from Mr. Collins. The letter begins with con-gratulations on Jane's engagement, then goes on to warn Mr. Bennet most seriously that he should on no account allow Elizabeth to accept a proposal from Dar-cy. The idea of Darcy proposing to Elizabeth strikes Mr. Bennet as a towering joke. Mr. Collins goes on to say that Lady Catherine would never consent to such a match.

At last Mr. Bennet notices that Elizabeth does not seem to be enjoying the joke. "For what do we live, but to make sport for our neighbors, and laugh at them in our turn?" he asks. Elizabeth tries to laugh. Her father then asks why Lady Catherine called. Was it to refuse her consent?

Elizabeth brushes this guess aside with another laugh, but it is too close for comfort. She goes away wondering about her own judgment. Her father is so sharp in his observations, and yet he believes it impossible that Darcy could be attracted to her. Does her father see too little? She wonders. Or has she been imagining too much?

CHAPTER FIFTY-EIGHT

Darcy does not send excuses, as Elizabeth had fear-fully expected. Instead he returns, and the very next morning after his arrival at Netherfield, he comes call-ing with Bingley. They all take a walk, but Jane and Bingley soon drop far behind, and Kitty stops at Lucas Lodge to visit Maria. Elizabeth and Darcy go on alone.

Taking courage, Elizabeth thanks him for his part in rescuing Lydia. He is surprised that Mrs. Gardiner could not be trusted with the secret. She quickly tells him the truth: it was Lydia who in her thoughtless way let it slip. He says, "If you will thank me, let it be for yourself alone . . . I believe I thought only of you."

With this excellent beginning, he goes on to tell her that his feelings toward her have not changed. But if she still doesn't want him, she has only to say so and he will be silent on this subject forever. With no hesitation but much embarrassment, Elizabeth quickly assures him that *her* feelings toward *him* have indeed changed, and she now hears his proposal with gratitude and joy.

Happy at last, the lovers walk on, freely sharing their thoughts and emotions over the happenings of the past several weeks. Darcy tells Elizabeth that Lady Catherine did indeed call on him to deliver her arguments against Elizabeth. But the effect was the opposite of what she intended. Her angry account of her visit—of every word she and Elizabeth exchanged—gave him hope that he might yet win Elizabeth's hand.

Both now admit that they have been heartily ashamed of what they said to each other on the memorable evening in Hunsford parsonage, when he made his offer of marriage and she rejected it. Darcy now tells her of his own self-examination since that night when she astonished him—not only with her refusal but with her strict criticism of his behavior. He grew up a loved and spoiled child, an only child for his first dozen years, he explains. He was brought up with good principles, but became proud and conceited—until his dear Elizabeth taught him otherwise.

When he first encountered her at Pemberley, he says, he had intended only to show her that he had changed his attitudes and manners. But within half an hour he was wishing for her to return his love.

Finally, he acknowledges that he had no trouble persuading Bingley to go back to Jane. He simply apologized for his interference and assured Bingley that Jane was not indifferent to him. Elizabeth is tempted to joke about Bingley's willingness to be guided by his friend. But she realizes that Darcy is not yet accustomed to being laughed at and wisely restrains her impulse.

CHAPTER FIFTY-NINE

Elizabeth's immediate problem is how to break her extraordinary news to her family. She knows that no one except Jane likes Darcy, and she blames this on herself for having expressed her own dislike of him so freely in the past.

She tells Jane her news that night, but the astonished sister can't believe it. Elizabeth is shaken. If Jane doesn't believe her, who will? To cover her dismay, she at first tells Jane that she began to love Darcy when she saw Pemberley. Then, becoming serious, she assures Jane that her change of feelings has come in response to everything that has happened. Very gradually, she explains, her initial prejudice gave way to understanding, appreciation, and finally love. She tells Jane of Darcy's part in the Lydia-Wickham affair, and the two sisters spend half the night talking.

The next day Bingley arrives, and by the warmth of his greeting Elizabeth can see that Darcy has told him of their engagement. Darcy is with him, and Mrs. Bennet asks Elizabeth to take him out for a walk again. She apologizes for making Elizabeth spend time with "that disagreeable man," but explains it is for Jane.

That evening Darcy visits Mr. Bennet in his study to ask his consent, and soon Mr. Bennet sends for Elizabeth. He is greatly troubled. He has given his consent, but he warns Elizabeth against marrying a man whom she cannot respect.

Elizabeth reassures him that she not only likes Darcy, she loves him. She explains the gradual change of her feelings and the events that changed them, then tells her father the whole story of how Darcy secretly rescued Lydia, managed her marriage, and paid out large sums to clear Wickham's past and insure his future. Amazed at all this, Mr. Bennet admits that Darcy deserves Elizabeth. He is happy that the expenditure of money on Lydia's behalf was Darcy's and not his brother-in-law's. "I shall offer to pay him . . . he will rant and storm about his love for you, and there will be an end of the matter."

Elizabeth has one more scene to face, her mother's reaction to her news. This she attends to in private, to spare Darcy. At first, Mrs. Bennet is as still as if she'd been turned to stone, but then she reacts exactly as Elizabeth had expected: she is overjoyed that Elizabeth has found such a rich husband. Elizabeth has some momentary forebodings about her mother's future behavior to Darcy. Fortunately, though, Mrs. Bennet is in such awe of her prospective son-in-law that she is hardly able to utter a word to him when they meet the next day. Mr. Bennet quips to Elizabeth that Wickham is still his favorite son-in-law, but he expects to like her husband quite as well as Jane's.

CHAPTER SIXTY

In a playful mood, Elizabeth asks Darcy to account for falling in love with her. He cannot: he was in love before he realized it, he says. She says he loved her for her "impertinence." He calls it the "liveliness of her mind." She surmises that he was disgusted with women who fussed over him and that he noticed her because she was different—she did not give him the flattery he was accustomed to. He might have hated her for that, she says, but because he was really good-hearted he loved her instead.

She is pleased with her explanation, but troubled because their happiness stems from a broken confidence: she thanked him for his kindness to Lydia, about which she should have known nothing. He reassures her that he meant to propose to her again anyway, because his aunt's interference had given him new hope.

He sits down at once to write Lady Catherine, telling her of his engagement. Another letter goes out that day, from Mr. Bennet to Mr. Collins, announcing Elizabeth's engagement to Darcy. Mr. Bennet advises Collins to console Lady Catherine as best he can, and counsels him to stand by Darcy, who has more patronage to give.

The Collinses arrive at Lucas Lodge. Charlotte has wisely decided to stay away from Hunsford awhile to escape Lady Catherine's rage. Despite her husband's disapproval, she calls to rejoice in Elizabeth's happiness.

Elizabeth's life is about to change dramatically, and she is painfully aware of how her family and her neighbors must appear to Darcy: Mr. Collins is so excessive and self-important in his expressions of respect, Sir William Lucas is so long-winded with his compliments, and Aunt Philips is so vulgar. But Darcy bears it all with surprising grace, a good omen for her future happiness with him.

CHAPTER SIXTY-ONE

The novel ends with a glimpse of the characters' later lives. Regretfully, the happy marriages of Jane and Elizabeth do not make Mrs. Bennet any more sensible. She remains hopelessly silly and subject to her imagined attacks of nerves. Mr. Bennet, missing Elizabeth, is a frequent visitor to Pemberley.

Bingley and Jane soon find Netherfield too near to Longbourn, and Bingley purchases an estate within thirty miles of Pemberley. Kitty spends much time visiting her sisters, and getting away from home proves good for her. Mary remains mostly at home, her mother's chief companion.

Lydia writes to Elizabeth, wishing her joy and hoping for financial help from Darcy. Elizabeth puts an end to that hope, but she and Jane do send the pair money out of their allowances. Lydia and Wickham move frequently and need help each time to pay accumulated debts from the previous residence. As anticipated, their affection for each other soon wanes, and their characters do not improve. Darcy does not receive Wickham at Pemberley, but he continues to help him privately, for Elizabeth's sake.

Caroline Bingley puts aside her disappointment at Darcy's marriage and becomes civil to Elizabeth, for the sake of still being welcome at Pemberley. Lady Catherine was so insulting to Elizabeth that Darcy broke off his relationship with his aunt, but Elizabeth persuades him to attempt a reconciliation. Her ladyship eventually condescends to visit Pemberley, out of curiosity, she says, to see how Elizabeth conducts herself.

Except for Jane and Bingley, the Gardiners remain the favorite relatives of both Darcy and Elizabeth, loved for themselves and also as the ones who made possible their happy ending.

A STEP BEYOND

Tests and Answers

TESTS

Test 1

1. What is one of the major themes of *Pride and Prejudice?* _____
   - A. Women's rights
   - B. Making a good marriage
   - C. Middle-class morality
   - D. Aristocratic manners

2. What is an entail? _____
   - A. The consequences of a decision
   - B. The award of the fox's tail to the leader of the hunt
   - C. The limitation of an inheritance to a specific line of heirs
   - D. An illegal claim to an estate

3. What attracts Darcy to Elizabeth Bennet? _____
   - A. Her fortune
   - B. Her beauty
   - C. Her social connections
   - D. Her lively mind

4. What argument by Darcy discourages Bingley from courting Jane Bennet? _____
   - A. Jane's apparent indifference to Bingley
   - B. Mrs. Bennet's indiscretions
   - C. The Bennet family's inferior social connections
   - D. The young Bennet girls' pursuit of the officers

5. Why does Charlotte Lucas marry Mr. _____
Collins?
   A. She loves him
   B. She is socially ambitious
   C. She is unhappy at home
   D. She wants security

6. Elizabeth criticizes her father as a husband _____
because he
   A. gambles
   B. makes fun of his wife
   C. is never at home
   D. drinks

7. Darcy's manner changes from haughty _____
coldness to courtesy and warmth to
   A. impress Caroline Bingley
   B. be accepted in society
   C. win Elizabeth's good opinion
   D. please Lady Catherine

8. Charlotte Brontë said that Jane Austen explored everything about her characters except their hearts. What did
she mean? Do you agree?

9. Is Charlotte Lucas right to marry Mr. Collins?

10. Good manners are of great importance in *Pride and Prejudice*. Do you think this emphasis is justified?

11. Privilege and responsibility are linked in *Pride and Prejudice*. What do you think of this linkage? Does it still
exist in our own times?

12. Judging by the marriages described in *Pride and Prejudice*, what do you think was Jane Austen's opinion of
marriage? Did she see it as a source of happiness?
Unhappiness? Was it a blessing, or a necessary evil?

Test 2

1. Wickham elopes with Lydia Bennet   _____
   A. because he loves her
   B. to have a woman companion
   C. for her fortune
   D. to make trouble for Darcy

2. When Mrs. Bennet learns of Lydia's _____
 elopement, she is most worried about
 Lydia's
   A. safety   B. health   C. reputation
   D. wedding clothes

3. Mr. Bennet says he likes Wickham best of his _____
 three sons-in-law because Wickham is
   A. rich   B. handsome   C. famous
   D. a scoundrel

4. Mr. Collins warns Mr. Bennet against letting _____
 Elizabeth marry Darcy because
   A. Darcy is untrustworthy
   B. Lady Catherine objects
   C. Elizabeth has no fortune
   D. Darcy does not love her

5. Jane and Bingley will make a happy marriage _____
 because they
   A. both like to dance
   B. are both given to quarreling
   C. have identical dispositions
   D. are both good-looking

6. A critic points out that Elizabeth and Darcy
 must "work their way" to love and marriage.
 Why?
   A. They hardly know each other
   B. They know each other too well
   C. They come from different classes of
     society

    D. They both have independent minds and
       partly mistaken opinions

7. Darcy says that Lady Catherine was _____
responsible for his second and successful
proposal of marriage to Elizabeth. How?
    A. By telling him what Elizabeth said, she
       gave him hope
    B. She gave her approval
    C. She praised Elizabeth
    D. She recommended the Bennet family

8. Jane Austen is noted for her treatment of relationships.
Discuss her handling of relationships in *Pride and Prejudice*.

9. Pride is the first word in Jane Austen's title. What is her
concept of this trait?

10. Like Darcy's pride, Elizabeth's prejudice undergoes a
sequence of change. Trace the progress of this
change.

11. *Pride and Prejudice* has been successfully adapted to the
theater, motion pictures, and television. What is the
quality of Jane Austen's skill that has made these dramatic adaptations so successful?

12. Some readers interpret *Pride and Prejudice* as a feminist
novel. Can you make an argument for this interpretation?

ANSWERS

Test 1

1. B   **2.** C   **3.** D   **4.** A   **5.** D   **6.** B
7. C

    8.   Charlotte Brontë's *Jane Eyre* and her sister Emily's
Wuthering Heights are leading examples of nineteenth century romantic novels, in which the characters undergo dramatic experiences and express intense passions and emo-

tions. Jane Austen lived under the classical restraints of the eighteenth century, when it was considered proper to keep passions and emotions under control. Brontë was scornful of this control, and of the attention to propriety and good manners in Austen's novels. But she can be proved wrong in saying that Austen did not write about her characters' hearts. As early as Chapter 6 we have evidence of jealousy in Caroline Bingley's spiteful remarks about Elizabeth Bennet's family. In Chapter 10 Jane Bennet suffers her first disappointment in Bingley's attentions and it is clear that she is seriously in love. The most revealing exposure of her characters' hearts, however, comes in Chapter 34, in the scene in Hunsford parsonage, when Darcy, much against his will, declares his love for Elizabeth, and Elizabeth tells him off in a burst of anger for his treatment of Jane and Wickham. In Darcy's letter (Chapter 35) strong feelings of bitterness, injury, and regret are mingled with love and longing for Elizabeth's good opinion. It is not difficult to show that, within the convention of her time and the restrictions of her own way of life, Jane Austen wrote eloquently about her characters' hearts.

9. You may answer this question either yes or no, and find evidence in the novel to support either position. If you agree with Elizabeth that Charlotte is wrong to marry a man she cannot respect, let alone love, you can back your opinion (in Chapter 22) by pointing out Elizabeth's shocked disbelief and her answer to Charlotte's defense of her decision. But note that Elizabeth has to change her opinion somewhat (Chapter 28) when she sees Charlotte's unobtrusive but ingenious arrangements to keep her ridiculous husband out of her way, and when she observes Charlotte's contentment with the hardwon security of an independent household of her own. This is an opportunity to expand on the lot of women in Jane Austen's class and time, who often had to make such hard choices as Charlotte's. You might note, on the opposing side, that Jane Austen and her sister Cassan-

dra both chose spinsterhood and were apparently contented with their choice, from the evidence of Jane's cheerful
letters.

10. You can make a case for good manners in the serious sense in which Jane Austen treats them. In recent years
young people have been scornful of manners as boring, artificial, and hypocritical. But every society has had its rules of
social behavior, even the rough, pioneer society of the
American Wild West. Jane Austen's world was pretty well
dominated by such social forms as paying calls, making conversation, avoiding painful subjects. In *Pride and Prejudice*
she shows how necessary these forms are as a kind of oil
that smooths relationships and makes for consideration of
others' feelings. Notice (in Chapter 45) during the morning
call of Elizabeth and Mrs. Gardiner at Pemberley that Georgiana's companion is the one who keeps a polite conversation going, covering for Georgiana's shyness, and that Caroline Bingley violates good manners by her malicious
remark about the officers, causing pain both to Darcy and
his sister. But note also that when Austen's characters break
the rules, it is either to reveal strong feelings, as in Caroline
Bingley's case, or for the sake of comedy, as when Lady
Catherine de Bourgh pries into the Bennet family arrangements in order to criticize them in her bossy way (Chapter
29). Mr. Collins' bowing and scraping (Chapters 14 and 18)
are examples of good manners that have been carried to a
ridiculous extreme. Your essay will give you an opportunity
to explore good manners either as a form of civilized consideration for others, or as a cover for hypocrisy and social
deceit. You will not find support for this latter judgment in
Pride and Prejudice, however, because Jane Austen never saw
good manners that way.

11. In the character of Darcy, Jane Austen gives us an
example of the privileged life of the well-to-do landed gentry of her time. As Darcy's character unfolds, it becomes

clear that privilege brings with it responsibility. Jane Austen was an accurate reporter of the society in which she lived. In eighteenth and nineteenth century England, the upper class of wealthy and educated men took over the responsibilities not only for government, but for charity, social welfare, and social reform. In *Pride and Prejudice* this responsibility becomes part of the story when Darcy's housekeeper (in Chapter 43), showing Elizabeth and the Gardiners through Pemberley, tells of his generous treatment of his servants and tenants, and Elizabeth muses on how many people's happiness lies within his guardianship. Darcy's sense of responsibility impresses her with his worth. Can you see a connection between modern philanthropies, foundations, art museum and university bequests by people of great wealth with this eighteenth century linkage of privilege and responsibility?

12.   While the theme of her novel is getting her young women married, Jane Austen, unlike the romantic novelists, was not content to end her story with "And they lived happily ever after" but dared to examine the institution of marriage itself. She gives us five married couples, all different. The first, Mr. and Mrs. Bennet, are introduced on the very first page and reappear throughout the novel. Mr. Bennet is the type of a husband who uses his feather-brained wife as a source of wry amusement. Even Elizabeth, who loves her father, admits to herself that his lack of respect for his marriage partner is a serious fault in a husband (Chapters 36, 42). Charlotte Lucas, married to Mr. Collins, wins Elizabeth's admiration for her management of her ridiculous husband, but hers is obviously a marriage of security rather than of happiness. Lydia's marriage to Wickham, a necessity to restore her respectability in society's eyes, soon loses all pretense of affection and deteriorates into the shallow relationship expected of two such irresponsible characters. (Chapter 61). As for the two romantic marriages, Jane to

Bingley and Elizabeth to Darcy, Mr. Bennet makes his ironic predictions (Chapter 59), and the novel closes with brief accounts of their happiness. The two marriages are different in quality but still both successful. What conclusions can you draw about Jane Austen's opinion of marriage? It seems that the success of a marriage in Austen's would—as perhaps in ours—depends on the characters of the married pair and the motives that brought them together in the first place.

Test 2

1. B   **2.** D   **3.** D   **4.** B   **5.** C   **6.** D
7. A

8. Not only the marriage relationship (see previous question) but other relationships both within the family and outside it have a strong role in the novel. Elizabeth may disapprove of her father (Chapters 36, 42) and try to correct her mother's embarrassing behavior (Chapter 18), but never does she disobey or have a rebellious thought toward her parents. Her sisterly relationship with Jane (Chapters 4, 40) is gently teasing but deeply considerate, reflecting perhaps Jane Austen's own relationship with her sister Cassandra. The aunt and niece relationship between Elizabeth and Mrs. Gardiner is especially interesting for its delicate balance of confidence and tact on both sides (Chapters 25, 44, 46, 51 and 52). Note that Jane Austen had a similarly close relationship with her nieces and nephews, at least according to her letters and their memoirs of her. Finally there are the friendships, particularly between Elizabeth and Charlotte, in which both can speak their minds without offense (Chapters 6, 22); and between Bingley and Darcy, two sharply contrasting characters (Chapter 10) who yet treat each other with mutual regard. Significant in the story development is Darcy's misguided but fatherly effort to keep Bingley from marrying Jane. When Darcy's opinion changes, Bingley is again willing to follow his guidance and renew the interrupted courtship. "A most convenient friend," Elizabeth muses (Chapter 58), but only to herself: Darcy is not yet ready to be laughed at. When they are married, Darcy's sister Georgiana is amazed that Elizabeth can tease Darcy and make him laugh at himself, a privilege (Chapter 61) that a wife may take but not a younger sister. With this final subtle touch Jane Austen shows her mastery of the art of relationships.

9. The pride to which the title refers is of course Darcy's, and one of the strengths of the novel is the way in which the concept of pride evolves. Its first impact (Chapter 3) is of Darcy's haughty behavior at the Meryton assembly, where no woman is handsome enough for him to dance with. Pride is identified there with arrogance, insolence, and conceit. Charlotte Lucas comments (Chapter 5) that with his wealth, family name and social status, Darcy has a *right* to be proud. This was probably a generally held opinion, but it was not, apparently, Jane Austen's. In his proposal to Elizabeth (Chapter 34), Darcy expresses pride in belonging to a superior social class, and he is astonished that she rejects him. His letter defending his actions toward Jane and Wickham (Chapter 35) is motivated not by pride so much as by a sense of moral obligation. He has put aside all thoughts of class and status, and expresses only criticism of the behavior of Elizabeth's family—criticism which Elizabeth must accept as just. Elizabeth (Chapter 50) believes that Darcy is too morally proud to renew his proposal of marriage now that Wickham is part of her family—no one as "correct" as Darcy would accept that scoundrel as a brother-in-law. Pride plays a role in Darcy's rescue of Lydia (Chapter 52) and in his management of her marriage—pride in the sense of taking responsibility for another person's welfare. Darcy's pride assumes another, very romantic dimension when he tries to keep his help to Lydia a secret from Elizabeth, so that he can win not her gratitude but her love.

10. Darcy's behavior on his first appearance (Chapter 3) surely gives Elizabeth just cause for her prejudice, but she dismisses it with a quip (Chapter 5). She becomes genuinely hostile to him only for the sake of others: first on Wickham's account (Chapters 16, 24, 26) and then on Jane's (Chapter 33). She shows great prejudice against him when she rejects his proposal (Chapter 34), but she begins to experience doubts about the justice of her thoughts as she reads and rereads his letter (Chapter 36). Although she remains angry with him for interfering with Jane's happiness, she begins her series of self-examinations, which we follow with a good deal of sympathy because she chides herself with humor rather than self-pity. She acknowledges that she has been prejudiced not only against Darcy but in favor of Wickham: one has all the goodness and the other all the appearance of it, she tells Jane, making fun of her own cleverness (Chapter 40). From then on her prejudice falls rapidly into shreds. The housekeeper's praise of Darcy, followed by his courtesy to the Gardiners and attentions to herself, blow away the last tatters of it. When at last he proposes again and she accepts him, her only regret is that she has expressed her dislike of him so freely in the past that Jane cannot believe she now loves him (Chapter 59). Still able to make fun of herself, she says she fell in love with him when she first saw Pemberley. But then she explains how prejudice gave way to understanding, appreciation, and finally love.

11. From the first page of the first chapter, Jane Austen demonstrates her extraordinary gift for developing her story and characters in dramatic scenes and sparkling dialogue. She does not tell us—she shows us. Here are some scenes you can refer to and describe as both comedy and drama: Chapter 1, the domestic scene at Longbourn; Chapter 6, confidences of Elizabeth and Charlotte; and Chapters 8 to 11, an almost continuous scene of social interplay and repartee among Darcy, Elizabeth, Bingley, and his sister Caroline.

Both the scene where Collins proposes (Chapter 19); and where Darcy proposes (Chapter 34) are famous in the dramatized versions, one for its comedy, the other for its impassioned confrontation between the embattled lovers. Lady Catherine's outrageous visit (Chapter 56) is only one of several comic scenes that you can refer to in your discussion of Jane Austen's gift for drama.

12.   In 1797, when Jane Austen wrote *Pride and Prejudice*, the right of women to vote was still more than a hundred years away but there were stirrings of protest. Mary Wollstonecraft published the first great feminist document, *A Vindication of the Rights of Women*, in 1792, and it created an uproar. News of this document may or may not have filtered down to young Jane in her father's parsonage at Steventon; that is something we may never know. Still, the insecure situation of middle-class women seems to have been on Austen's mind when she came to write the novel. Although she turned the search for a husband into a comedy, we cannot doubt that she took very seriously the financial necessity of making a good marriage that confronted most women of her class. In *Pride and Prejudice*, Austen's concern for these women is best expressed through the character of Charlotte Lucas. Charlotte's attitude toward marriage (Chapters 6 and 22) shocks Elizabeth, who can only think of marriage as something based on affection and respect. But in her day, Charlotte's attitude was a practical approach to the realities of a young woman's life. Jane Bennet with her beauty and Elizabeth with her wit and charm might look forward to a marriage of love, but Charlotte is a plain girl, the eldest of a large family of modest means, and she can only hope for a marriage that will bring her security. By marrying Charlotte to such a ludicrous husband as Mr. Collins, Jane Austen serves the comic aspect of her novel, but she tells us something serious as well about the women of her day.

Term Paper Ideas

1. Charlotte Brontë said that Jane Austen wrote of everything about her characters except their hearts. What do you think she meant? Is Austen's presentation of her characters' emotions cold or superficial in any way? Do any of her characters express strong, deep emotions?

2. Why was a good marriage crucial to a woman in Jane Austen's day? Is that still true today? In what ways have women's lives changed? What problems—if any—do today's women still have in common with Jane Austen's characters?

3. What careers were open to middle-class English men in Jane Austen's day? Give examples of gentlemanly occupations in Austen's own family, as well as in *Pride and Prejudice*.

4. Sir Walter Scott admired Jane Austen as a "new" novelist. He said she wrote of common events with such spirit and originality that the reader did not miss the excitement of uncommon events. Critics nowadays call this "realism." Discuss Jane Austen's realism in *Pride and Prejudice*.

5. "Trade" and "landed property" are contrasted in *Pride and Prejudice*. The fortunes of the two good friends, Bingley and Darcy, come from separate sources—Bingley's from trade, Darcy's from property. Yet they are friends and social equals. This was a change from the past in England. Why? What was happening in the late eighteenth and early nineteenth century? Research this historical period and show how its social changes are reflected in the novel.

6. Although *Pride and Prejudice* is Jane Austen's best-known novel, some critics consider *Emma* or *Mansfield Park* her masterpiece. If you have read one of these novels, would you agree with this judgment? Compare the merits of either of these novels with *Pride and Prejudice*.

7. *Pride and Prejudice* is described as social comedy. What aspects of society is Jane Austen making fun of in this novel?

8. Jane Austen uses irony to great effect in her novels. Define the term irony and give examples from *Pride and Prejudice*.

9. Novels in Jane Austen's day were written mostly by women, and most often under assumed names. Why were so many women writing, and why did they hide their identity or, like Jane Austen, not sign their books at all? You will need to do research on the history of women writers to discuss this subject.

10. "Vulgar" and "mercenary" are words that some nineteenth-century critics used to describe Jane Austen's work. Why? Do you agree? Are any characters in *Pride and Prejudice* mercenary?

11. *Pride and Prejudice* has been dramatized for stage, screen, and television. Why? Describe some scenes that are written in dramatic form in the novel.

12. Five married couples are presented in *Pride and Prejudice:* Mr. and Mrs. Bennet, Charlotte and Mr. Collins, Lydia and Wickham, Jane and Bingley, Elizabeth and Darcy. No two of the marriages are alike. Describe some of their differences.

13. Elizabeth is shocked when her friend Charlotte accepts Mr. Collins's proposal of marriage. Why? How does Charlotte explain her decision? What do you think of her reasons?

14. Charlotte Lucas believes that happiness in marriage is pure chance. How does she explain this? Does Elizabeth agree? Which woman is the idealist? Explain.

15. Elizabeth says that she fell in love with Darcy when she first saw Pemberley. Is she serious? Judging from her self-examinations, what stages did her attitude toward him go through?

16. Darcy's pride—and Elizabeth's perception of it—goes through a series of evolutionary changes in the course of the novel. At first he seems arrogant and conceited—to Elizabeth and the reader. How does he change in the course of the novel? Is he still a proud man by the end of the novel? How has Elizabeth's perception of his pride changed?

17. Two characters in *Pride and Prejudice*, Mr. Collins and Lady Catherine de Bourgh, are famous as comic creations. Describe either or both of them.

18. Mr. and Mrs. Bennet are examples of Jane Austen's skill in character development—he for his wit, she for her foolishness. Describe them and their relationship, using examples from the novel.

19. Jane Austen's writing style was considered unusual for her time—an era of flowery descriptive writing and emotional excess. Give examples of her clear and concise prose.

20. Jane Austen, both in her own life and in *Pride and Prejudice*, made cheerfulness a social obligation. Keeping your troubles to yourself is a form of considerateness toward others. Can you find examples of this in Elizabeth's and Jane's behavior?

21. In his letter revealing the truth about Wickham, Darcy counts on Elizabeth to keep his revelations secret. Was this to spare Wickham? Or to protect the reputation of his young sister Georgiana?

22. Later on, Darcy also asks the Gardiners not to reveal his part in the rescue of Lydia. Here his motive is different. What is it?

23. What does Lady Catherine hope to accomplish in her visit to Elizabeth? Does she succeed?

24. How does Lady Catherine inadvertently bring about Darcy's second proposal of marriage to Elizabeth?

25.   Wickham seems to be the only truly wicked character in *Pride and Prejudice*. Is he in fact so wicked? Or does he merely illustrate the difficulty of getting along in that society without money?

Further Reading

CRITICAL WORKS

Jane Austen: Bicentenary Essays, edited by John Halperin. Cambridge: Cambridge University Press, 1975.

Cecil, David. *A Portrait of Jane Austen*. New York: Hill and Wang, 1980.

Cecil, Lord David. *Jane Austen*. Cambridge: Cambridge University Press, 1935.

Hardwick, Michael. *A Guide to Jane Austen*. New York: Scribner's, 1982.

Litz, A. Walton. *Jane Austen: A Study of Her Artistic Development*. Oxford: Oxford University Press, 1965.

Mudrick, Marvin. *Jane Austen: Irony as Defense and Discovery*. Princeton: Princeton University Press, 1952.

Rees, Joan. *Jane Austen, Woman and Writer*. New York: St. Martin's, 1976.

Villard, Léonie. *Jane Austen, A French Appreciation*, translated by Veronica Lucas. New York: Dutton, 1924.

Wright, Andrew H. *Jane Austen's Novels, A Study in Structure*. Oxford: Oxford University Press, 1953.

AUTHOR'S OTHER WORKS

1. *Sense and Sensibility*. Published in 1811, two years before *Pride and Prejudice*, it was the first of Jane Austen's novels to appear in print. As with all her novels, the background is country society. The story moves briefly to London, but nothing is made of the town scene. Elinor and Marianne Dashwood are two young sisters of contrasting personalities. Elinor represents the *sense* of the title; she has a strong grasp of reality, a respect for conventional social behavior, and such good control of her feelings that she appears cold. Marianne stands for *sensibility*, an old-fashioned word that means a tendency both to feel and to express the emotions. Today we would call a person like

Marianne "oversensitive." Disappointed in love, she becomes seriously ill. Elinor, also disappointed in love, conceals her suffering so well that no one knows of it. In the end both sisters marry happily. The drive to marry for money is not central to the novel, but it is a strong undercurrent—in this novel it is a more powerful drive for the young men than for the young women. Obviously this was a preoccupation of both sexes in Jane Austen's social class.

2.   *Mansfield Park.* Published in 1814, this is the story of a gentle and self-effacing girl, Fanny Price, who is taken as a child from her parents' large, impoverished family to grow up in the home of her well-to-do uncle and aunt, Sir Thomas and Lady Bertram of Mansfield Park. They have two handsome, self-centered daughters, a son who is their heir and who cares only for hunting and racehorses, and a second son, Edmund, the only one sympathetic to Fanny. The Bertrams become involved with a fashionable brother and sister, Henry and Mary Crawford. This involvement leads to the disgrace of one of the daughters and a heart-searching disappointment for Edmund. In the end Edmund realizes that Fanny is the right wife for him, and Fanny, who has loved him from the first, is happy at last. A central part of the story is devoted to a project in amateur theatricals, in which Jane Austen brilliantly reveals the characters and relationships of the young people. Some critics consider *Mansfield Park* her finest work.

3.   *Emma.* Published in 1916, this novel has more critical votes than *Mansfield Park* as Jane Austen's masterpiece. As a study of a single character and her interaction with the people of her country village, it has a striking unity of action and character development. Twenty-year-old Emma Woodhouse, "handsome, clever, and rich," the mistress of her widowed father's house, takes under her wing a girl without family, pretty Harriet Smith. This leads Emma into a match-making project that backfires not only on Harriet but on Emma herself, with some grief and much comedy. Mr.

Knightley, a bachelor in his thirties, master of a large estate nearby, is Emma's friend and severest critic, whose love for her she does not recognize or return until near the novel's end. A subplot involves Emma with beautiful Jane Fairfax—whose lack of fortune condemns her to the life of a governess-companion—and with an attractive, somewhat spoiled young man who has been adopted by wealthy childless relatives. In its detailed comedy-drama of a small society within a narrow frame, *Emma* is the perfect example of Jane Austen's own description of her art as a painter of miniatures, the fashionable tiny portraits of the period, painted on small pieces of ivory with a very fine brush.

4. *Northanger Abbey.* Published in 1818, the year after Jane Austen's death, in combination with *Persuasion* and a biographical preface on the author by her brother Henry Austen. This is a pure comedy, the story of a wholesome young girl, Catherine Morland, whose head is full of the terrifying adventures of the day's Gothic novels. Invited to stay at the abbey, she is disappointed to find no hidden chambers or secret passages in the modernized manor house, and her fantasy, fed on popular fiction, takes off in wild imaginings about the sudden death suffered by her friend Eleanor Tilney's mother. Eleanor's brother Henry, a witty, charming young clergyman attracted to Catherine, firmly sets her right. She is suddenly and inconsiderately sent home by the Tilneys' tyrannical father, who has discovered that he was deceived in believing that Catherine had prospects of a fortune. Henry at once rides after her, proposes, and is accepted. As rector of a good "living" (see the glossary) he is independent, but Catherine's father, also a clergyman, while pleased with Henry, will not give his consent until General Tilney consents. Fortunately, Eleanor marries the man of her choice, who has come into a fortune and a title; General Tilney forgives Catherine for not being an heiress; and Catherine and Henry are married. Even though it wasn't published until after her death, *Northanger*

Abbey was actually Jane Austen's first effort at a full-length novel—and it still bears some traces of having been a youthful work. With the family's stay in Bath after the Reverend Austen's retirement, she was able to set part of her novel in this fashionable setting and add a subplot involving an opportunistic sister and brother who deceive Catherine, her own brother, and the Tilneys' irascible father. The novel is generally considered Jane Austen's parody of the horror novels of her time.

5. *Persuasion.* Published in 1818, this is Jane Austen's last and tenderest novel, the story of a love affair that, unlike most love affairs, has a second chance. Anne Elliot is the middle daughter of Sir Walter Elliot of Kellynch Hall, a vain and foolish baronet. The oldest daughter—handsome, snobbish Elizabeth—is unmarried at twenty-nine, while the youngest, Mary—a fretful and complaining young mother—is the wife of a local squire's son. Anne at nineteen was persuaded to break off her engagement to Frederick Wentworth, a young naval officer without fortune or prospects. Eight years have passed since then as the novel opens. Captain Wentworth has become wealthy, and he is again nearby, staying with relatives and looking for a wife. Anne still loves him, but he is still unforgiving. Through the working out of several subplots, the love of eight years past turns out to be constant in both the lovers, and the novel is brought to a happy end. Much of this story takes place in Bath, and the fashionable resort setting is treated with far more sophistication here than in *Northanger Abbey*. Similarly, the scheming of snobs and opportunists is more subtle than in the earlier novel. Some of the most engaging characters in *Persuasion* are naval officers and their wives. For these, and for her attractive hero, Jane Austen drew lovingly on what she knew of the Navy and naval people's life ashore from her two sailor brothers, both of whom became admirals in the Napoleonic Wars.

Glossary

Assembly   A community ball or dance held in a public ball-room, as distinct from a private ball held at someone's home.

Entail   The limitation of the inheritance of a landed estate to a specific line of heirs. Usually this meant a male heir, as in the case of Mr. Bennet's estate of Longbourn. The entail can be broken by the heir, on coming of age, voluntarily joining with the owner of the estate in a legal proceeding. An entail may have been laid down in some ancestor's will, generations earlier, as Mrs. Bennet was never able to understand.

In Trade   A way of earning one's income that is middle-class but not at as high a level in society as having landed property. "Trade" could mean manufacturing, any form of business or commerce, or the practice of law.

A Living   Specifically in England, an appointment as rector to a Church of England parish with whatever income was attached to it, including a house called the *rectory* or *parsonage*. Jane Austen's father, the Reverend George Austen, held two neighboring and very small livings; his income from them was so small that he was obliged to take in pupils in order to support his large family. A good living, such as several mentioned in Jane Austen's novels, and in particular the living that was in the Darcy family's power to give, might yield a very comfortable income.

Marriage Settlement   The sum settled on a woman, usually by her spouse or father, when she married. Her children were entitled to share this sum on her death.

Wedding Clothes   The wardrobe and linens that a bride acquires for her married life and household. We use the French word, *trousseau*, for this. Lydia's wedding clothes are Mrs. Bennet's main concern when she learns that Lydia has eloped.

The Critics

A talent for describing ordinary life

[I have] read again, and for the third time at least, Miss Austen's very finely written novel of *Pride and Prejudice.* That young lady had a talent for describing the involvements, and feelings, and characters of ordinary life, which is to me the most wonderful I ever met with. The Big Bow-wow strain I can do myself like any now going; but the exquisite touch, which renders ordinary commonplace things and characters interesting, from the truth of the description and the sentiment, is denied to me. What a pity such a gifted creature died so early!

> *Sir Walter Scott,* Diary, *1826*

"Nearest to the manner" of Shakespeare

Shakespeare has had neither equal nor second. But among the writers who . . . have approached nearest to the manner of the great master, we have no hesitation in placing Jane Austen, a woman of whom England is justly proud. She has given us a multitude of characters, all in a certain sense, commonplace, all such as we meet every day. Yet they are all as perfectly discriminated from each other as if they were the most eccentric of human beings.

> *Lord Macaulay,* Edinburgh Review, *1843*

"Why do you like Miss Austen so very much?"

Why do you like Miss Austen so very much? I am puzzled on that point. What induced you to say that you would have rather written *Pride and Prejudice* . . . than any of the Waverley Novels?

I had not seen *Pride and Prejudice* till I read that sentence of yours, and then I got the book. And what did I find? An accurate daguerreotyped portrait of a commonplace face; a carefully fenced, highly cultivated garden, with neat borders and delicate flowers; but no glance of a bright, vivid physiognomy, no open country, no fresh air, no blue hill, no bonny beck. I should hardly like to live with her ladies and gentlemen, in their elegant but confined houses.

> *Charlotte Brontë, in a letter to George Henry Lewes, 1848*

"Truth is never sacrificed . . ."

Miss Austen is, of all his successors, the one who most nearly resembles Richardson in the power of impressing reality upon her characters. There is a perfection in the exhibition of Miss Austen's characters which no one else has approached; and truth is never for an instant sacrificed in that delicate atmosphere of satire which pervades her works. . . .

. . . She has been accused of writing dull stories about ordinary people. But her supposed ordinary people are really not such very ordinary people. Let any one who is inclined to criticise on this score endeavour to construct from among the ordinary people of his own acquaintance one character that shall be capable of interesting any reader for ten minutes. It will then be found how great has been the discrimination of Miss Austen in the selection of her characters and how skilful is her treatment of them.

> *W. F. Pollock*, Fraser's Magazine, 1860

"Largest claims . . . in our own time . . ."

It should not be surprising that the largest claims for Jane Austen's art have been made in our own time. The success of modern criticism in analyzing works of fiction by methods formerly associated with the study of lyric poetry has made the traditional objections to Jane Austen's limited subject-matter seem almost irrelevant. By emphasizing her control of language and mastery of ironic exposure, recent critics have greatly expanded our appreciation of what Jane Austen accomplished on her "little bit (two Inches wide) of Ivory."

> *A. Walton Litz*, Jane Austen: A Study of Her Artistic Development, 1965

"A philosophy of life . . ."

In these novels, which do not confine their psychological study to principles and formulae, but present it in their elements of variety, individuality and personality, we are given a philosophy of life. A philosophy which though amiable in appearance is none the less dogmatic, and leaves no place for uneasiness or doubt in the author, who puts it into practice and exhibits it in her novels.

The peace, ease and well-being of outer circumstances corresponds with the inner atmosphere of moral serenity, tranquility, and contentment.

An artist less sure of herself, a less skilful psychologist, would try to create this double atmosphere by affirming that peace and joy are laws of life.

Jane Austen affirms nothing of the kind; she contents herself with proving it. . . .

. . . Because she herself has experienced the kindness of life which has never imposed unbearable sufferings upon her, because she dares to look the contradictions, absurdities and follies which appear on the surface of things, in the face and always with a smile, she has an unshakable confidence in life, an absolute certainty that the unknown power which governs the world desires order and well-being in all things.

Her confidence in life is not due solely to the absence of any bitter trials, it is also the result of a natural leaning to that equilibrium of the spirit, unstable perhaps, but always regained after temporary loss, which we call optimism.

Here, again, Jane Austen is in advance of her time and beyond the region of romantic disquietude, and realizes in the clear atmosphere of her narrow sphere something of the modern "will to live." . . .

Léonie Villard, Jane Austen, A French Appreciation, *1924*

"Jane Austen would have been surprised. . . ."

If I am surprised to find myself lecturing to you, Jane Austen would have been still more surprised to find herself being lectured about. For—it is the most striking fact discovered by her life history— she did not take her work very seriously.

Hers was no career of solemn and solitary self-dedication. Neat, elegant and sociable, she spent most of her day sitting in the drawing-room of the parsonage which was her home, sewing and gossiping. From time to time, it is said, she would begin to laugh, and then, stepping across to the writing-table, she would scribble a few lines on a sheet of paper. But if visitors called she slipt the pages under the blotter; when the pages had accumulated into a story, she let it lie for years in a drawer unread. And when at last it did emerge to the public gaze, she refused in the slightest degree to modify the conventional order of her life to suit with the character of a professional authoress. As for the applause of posterity, she seems never to have given it a moment's thought: it was no part of her sensible philosophy to worry about admiration that she would not live to enjoy.

Yet one hundred and nineteen years have passed since her death, and yearly the applause of posterity has grown louder. . . . All discriminating critics admire her books, most educated readers enjoy them; her fame, if not highest among English novelists, is of all the most secure. . . . Jane Austen was a comedian. Her first literary impulse was humorous; and to the end of her life humour was an integral part of her creative process: as her imagination starts to function a smile begins to spread itself across her features. And the smile is the signature on the finished work. It is the angle of her satiric vision, the light of her wit that gives its peculiar glitter and proportion to her picture of the world.

Lord David Cecil, Jane Austen, *1935*

"To treat life as comedy . . ."

Distance—from her subject and from the reader—was Jane Austen's first condition for writing. . . . Her temperament chose irony at once: she maintained her distance by diverting herself and

her audience with an unengaged laughter, by setting irony, the instrument—and, as it happened,
the genius—of her temperament, to sharpen and
expose all the incongruities between form and fact,
all the delusions intrinsic to conventional art and
conventional society.

If Jane Austen's irony appears at times almost
inhumanly cold and penetrating, . . . it may be
because we are accustomed to the soft or senti-
mental alloying of most irony. Sympathy is irrelevant to irony. Jane Austen's compulsion, and
genius, is to look only for incongruity; and it
delights her wherever she finds it. . . .

It was Jane Austen's first choice to treat life,
even in her letters, as material for comedy: not
sentimentally, not morally, indeed not tied to any
train of consequences, but with a detached discrimination among its incongruities. She was
interested in a person, an object, an event, only as
she might observe and recreate them free of consequences, as performance, as tableau: her frame
was comedy, her defining artistic impulse was irony. Compulsion was also, or became, art. Every-
where she found incongruities between overt and
hidden, between professed and acted upon, failures of wholeness which in life have consequences
and must be judged but in comedy—and for Jane
Austen—are relieved of guilt and responsibility at
the moment of perception, to be explored and pro-
gressively illuminated by irony.

> *Marvin Mudrick*, Jane Austen: Irony
> as Defense and Discovery, *1952*

"An embarrassing position in literary history . . ."

Jane Austen occupies an embarrassing position
in literary history—embarrassing because never
for a moment does she accommodate herself to the
facile generalizations which are made about her
contemporaries. Wordsworth and Coleridge can,
though with some inaccuracy, be called Romantic;
they were both born within five years of Jane Austen. But she is too little a writer of the nineteenth
century to be called Romantic, too much a person

of her time to be called Classic, too original and too great to be considered a precursor or an apotheosis: she is, however much indebted to her literary forebears . . ., unique. Working with materials extremely limited in themselves, she develops themes of the broadest significance; the novels go beyond social record . . . to moral concern, perplexity, and commitment.

The spinster daughter of a country parson, Jane Austen not only limits herself to the sphere which she understands, she even picks and chooses amongst the raw materials of experience available to her, eschewing what her genius cannot control: '3 or 4 Families in a Country Village is the very thing to work on,' she writes to her niece.

Andrew H. Wright, Jane Austen's
Novels: A Study in Structure, *1953*